The Ghosts of Devils Lake

True Stories from My Haunted Hometown

Copyright

The Ghosts of Devils Lake is © 2013 by Corrine Kenner. All rights reserved.

This book contains material protected under international and federal copyright laws and treaties. Any unauthorized reprint or use of this material is prohibited. No part of this book may be reproduced or transmitted in any form or by any means, electronic or mechanical, including photocopying, recording, or by any information storage and retrieval system, without express written permission from the author.

ISBN 978-1492918110

Cover imagery by Jill Battaglia

The historic photos in this book are in the public domain.

Additional Copies

To order additional copies of this book, visit www.GhostsOfDevilsLake.com

Contact Information

If you have comments, suggestions, corrections, or additions for future editions of this book, email corrine@corrinekenner.com

Dedication

To my parents, Wayne and Carolyn Kenner, who always said my writing would take me places.

Contents

Introduction	1
The Ghostly Legend of Devils Lake	3
The Song of Howastena	7
The History of Devils Lake	8
The Museum Ghost	10
Officer Sneesby's Last Patrol	15
The Lightman at the Opera House	17
The Maiden on the Cliff	19
The Ghost Wife	23
The Haunting of Mary Berri Chapman	28
Duncan Graham's Island	32
The Resurrection of Little Flower	35
Yellowstone Vic	40
Little Crow and the Indian Uprising	42
Alfred Sully's Game of Chance	46
Haunted Fort Totten	49
The Ghost of Pierre Bottineau	51
The Story of Brave Bear	54
The Grief of The Only One's Wife	60
The Men Who Fell with Custer	61
The Soldiers on the Staircase	63
Dear Brother: Michael Vetter's Letters	65
The Haunted Little Theatre	67
Little Fish and the Indians of Fort Totten	69
Ignatius Court and the Indian School	71
Rain in the Face	73
Mrs. Faribault's Fresh-Baked Bread	77
The Ghost of Grand Harbor	80
The Guardian of the Grand Army of the Republic	83
The Cowboy's Lament	85
The Devil's Heart	87
Chotanka, the Bear Man	89
The Animal People of Devil's Heart	93
The Devil's Tooth	96

The Little People of Devils Lake	99
The Dead Man's Trail	102
The Hired Man	104
The Murder of the Ward Brothers	109
The Blizzard Ghost	115
Horn Cloud's Revenge	119
The Virgin Feast	121
The Phantom Ship of Devils Lake	123
The Day Jack Kenny Lost His Head	125
The Devils Lake Sea Serpent	127
The War Maiden	130
The Stairway to Hell	133
The Haunted Train Station	135
The Wreck of the Oriental Express	138
The Ghosts at the Great Northern Hotel	140
The Water Witch of the West	143
The Vision of White Thunder	145
Sister Saint Alfred's Deathbed Revelations	149
The Edwards House	152
The Lost Tribe of Garske Colony	154
The Ghost of the *Minnie H*	159
The Earl of Caithness	163
Queen Victoria's Maid	167
The Odd Fellows Dance Hall	170
Buffalo Bones	174
The Devils Lake Ghost Tour	177
Sources	182
About the Author	189
Also by Corrine Kenner	190

The Legend of Minnewaukan

By the lake's yet heaving waters, on the rocks beside the strand,
Crouched the women, wildly wailing, one despairing, sobbing band:
For those waters now so smiling, tossing sportive at their feet,
Had in cruel wrath bereft them, had engulfed their homing feet.
Thus the death song each still ending, gazing wistful o'er the brine,
"Minnewaukan! Spirit Water! Cause of woe to me and mine!"
Stood the chieftain's dark-eyed daughter 'mid the women of her tribe.
Wild she gazed across those waters that nor tear nor vow could bribe.
As they mourned the ne'er returning, gave to grief an utterance free.
For a father wept Nadassa, for her love, for brethren three.
"Watha!" cried she, "Mighty hunter! Braves of a mighty line!
Whelmed in Meda's bitter waters, cruel e'er to me and mine!"
Dimmed her eyes see not the splendor of that wood embosomed gem.
Not the hills, blue in the distance, with their sylvan diadem,
Not the crested, sage-green waters, dancing in the westering sun,
Not a sunlit, stately pinewood, backed by rising vapors don;
But the dirge, with bitter wailing, sang she with the sun's decline,
"Minnewaukan! Haunted Water! Name of woe to me and mine!"

— Rena Percival

Introduction

I GREW UP near Devils Lake, surrounded by the ghosts of the area's past.

I mean that literally. My great-grandparents were Norwegian immigrants who planted their roots in the North Dakota soil. I was raised on the family farm they established, set among fields of wheat and sunflowers. From my bedroom window, on the second floor of the farmhouse my grandfather built, I could see the lake itself—covered with ice and snow in the winter, but shining and blue in the summer.

As a child, I learned firsthand that the area is haunted by the spirits of the people who settled the land—immigrants and Indians alike. I learned how they haunt the dusty trails they first walked more than a century ago, and how they're still seen in the shadows of the wooded shoreline.

In fact, Devils Lake might have more ghosts than people. Supernatural sightings and spectral visions have marked the region for as long as anyone can remember.

I grew up hearing many of the stories in this book. When I was younger, I thought they were simply myths and legends—tall tales, in short, to help make the long North Dakota winters more bearable. After all, Devils Lake is a remote and isolated place, hundreds of miles from any major city. The summers are brief and fleeting, and the winter's cold will literally take your breath away.

The shared history of the region gives people in the area a certain sense of camaraderie. Beyond the state's borders, however, most people have never heard the accounts you're about to read.

Most people would never believe them, either.

A few years ago, I started to research the local legends I had heard as a child. Imagine my surprise when I discovered that they were true. Even the oldest Indian tales, passed down through generations of storytellers, are based on actual events. The more recent reports are substantiated by state records, newspaper chronicles, and first-hand accounts.

While I've put my own spin on the stories, all of the accounts in this book are genuine; you'll find my sources and references listed in the back of the book.

Originally, these stories were told by firelight, in tipis, tents, sod huts, and cabins. Those who listened would take time to get comfortable first—sitting quietly on blankets, or buffalo robes, or handmade wooden chairs—and then they would wrap themselves completely in the words of the storytellers.

Before you turn the page, you should get comfortable, too. Find a quiet corner in a darkened room. Build a fire or light some candles. Sit still.

You're about to meet the Ghosts of Devils Lake.

— Corrine Kenner
Devils Lake, North Dakota
October 2013

The Ghostly Legend of Devils Lake

Devils Lake has always been associated with mysticism and mystery. In fact, the lake got its name because of a tragedy foretold by a holy man with visions of the future.

FOR MANY YEARS, Devils Lake was a calm and peaceful place, where Dakota Indians lived and enjoyed the bounty of nature.

There were countless quiet bays along the shoreline, filled with walleye and perch. There were stretches of prairie and swaths of forested land. Oaks and elms provided shade and shelter, and huge herds of buffalo roamed through the area, ensuring a steady supply of food, leather, and fur.

That's not to say that life along the shores of Devils Lake had always been idyllic. In fact, the Dakota people who made the area their home had discovered the lake under duress. Originally, they had been refugees, driven to the area after generations of war.

In earlier times, the Dakota people had lived a settled, agricultural life near the Great Lakes, hundreds of miles to the east. When French Canadian fur traders and trappers filtered into that area during the 1600s, the explorers happened to encounter the Ojibwe first. As the explorers and the Indians got to know each other, the Ojibwe told them about another band of Indians who lived further west: the hated *Nadouessioux.*

As it happens, *Nadouessioux* was the Ojibwe word for "enemy." It took many years for the French explorers to learn that the so-called "Sioux" actually called themselves the *Dakotas*—their word for "friends." By that time, however, it was too late for the Dakota people. The French had already traded guns for Ojibwe furs, and the Ojibwe had used those guns to drive their rivals west.

By 1750, some of the Dakota had started to filter into modern-day North Dakota, where they were the first people to settle the shores of Devils Lake. They called the new lake *Mini-wakan*—their words for "holy water." That phrase can also be translated as "Spirit Lake." That's the name the Dakota people still use for the lake, and for today's reservation nation on its southern shores.

The Dakotas spent the warmest months of the year along the shores of Spirit Lake, and then migrated south for the long, cold winters. They built tipis from tall, straight poplars, and covered them with bison hides. While the young men hunted bison, antelope, and bears, old men could remain in the camp and smoke their pipes. The women kept the fires going, and they gathered plums and berries with their children.

But one evening, a young Dakota hunter named Watha returned to the camp with a disturbing report. He had spotted some of their enemies, the Ojibwe, camped in the Turtle Mountains, a day's travel to the east.

With the news, the Dakota people decided that they wouldn't let history repeat itself. They refused to be driven off their land again. This time, the Dakota people were determined to hold their ground. There would be a war.

For weeks, everyone in the Dakota tribe prepared for battle. Boat builders carved canoes from dawn until dark. Other men made arrows and tomahawks, and the women ornamented them with beads and buckskin. The chief's daughter, Nadassa, was in love with the hunter Watha, and she made a special leather sheaf for his knife.

The only one who opposed the war was Owanda, the tribe's holy man and seer. He was a respected elder, in tune with nature and all the signs. He could read the weather. He could feel the vibrations of the future. He could see into the spirit world—and as preparations for battle scaled up around him, he was overwhelmed by portents of disaster.

"This is not a just war," he warned. "If we spill blood only in anger, we will suffer in return."

Watha, the hunter and scout, disagreed. He was a confident, strong young man—almost nude, actually, with little more than a strip of leather wound around his hips. His hair blew in the wind, and he always carried a weapon in his hand.

"We have to fight," he said. "We must protect our land."

Back then, before any tribe would head into battle, the holy man would make a tipi for himself and sit in it alone, looking into the future and seeing visions of the conflict. As he meditated, the members of the tribe would bring him offerings and gifts, and he would make holy emblems and charms to protect them in combat.

The visions that Owanda saw were terrifying. Lightning filled the sky, sending sparks through the air and setting fires on the ground. Warriors plummeted to their deaths, their bodies flailing, silhouetted against a black sky and gray clouds. Women wailed with grief, but their cries of anguish were drowned by a raging wind.

Owanda tried to persuade his people that they were making a terrible mistake, but no one would believe him.

He pointed to a series of bad omens: the geese and ducks that usually stayed to the north, for example, were all migrating far earlier than they had in other years. Owanda said they were fleeing to put as many miles as possible between themselves and the battle.

Owanda's people denied his assertions. Instead, they insisted that the early migration was a good sign, because the birds were a source of food. "The Great Spirit is sending them to us in time of need," they told him.

It wasn't quite autumn, so when the leaves turned red ahead of season, Owanda told the band that the blood of their warriors would run just as red. His people disagreed. "It's a sign of our victory," they declared.

Just before they headed off to battle, the warriors assembled in the center of camp. As tradition dictated, they sat in a circle outside the holy man's tent. Owanda walked toward them, singing a holy song, to give them the charms he had made and tell them their fate.

Hocoka wan cicuqon, he sang. *Yutonkal nunwe*.

In English, that meant, "In this circle, O ye warriors, lo, I tell you, each his future. All shall be as I now reveal it. In this circle, hear ye!"

Sadly, Owanda told the men that they would soon say goodbye to their loved ones for the last time. They wouldn't return from battle. Instead, they would be lost to the storms of time.

There was still time to call off the fight, he said—but the tribe couldn't be dissuaded. Even though they had seen the same omens Owanda had described, the warriors and their families simply decided that Owanda's interpretations were wrong.

On the morning they left, the sky was unusually bright and sunny. Owanda tried one last time to warn them that the glimmers of light that glinted off the surface of the water were glints of treachery—but the rest of the tribe said the stillness was simply more proof of the Great Spirit's approval.

The young men climbed into their canoes and paddled off across the lake.

After three days, those who stayed behind started to watch the lake for the warriors' return. Night came, but there was no sign of them.

Another day passed, and the air seemed ominously still. The leaves on the trees drooped in the heat, and the birds stopped singing. That evening, the sky turned a livid green, and gray clouds started to form along the western horizon.

Suddenly, the chief's daughter Nadassa shouted for joy: the men were returning!

Everyone raced to the lake, where they could see the warriors silhouetted against the setting sun. They could see scalps waving from the sides of the canoes. The message was clear: the Dakota people had been victorious, and their land was secure.

On shore, the families began to celebrate. They lit fires, filled pipes, and started to sing. They were happy to prove that Owanda had been wrong.

Before long, however, they realized that the boats seemed to be moving in slow motion. The warriors were rowing against a wind that was blowing stronger and stronger.

As they watched, Owanda's vision came true before their eyes.

Black clouds blew in. Lightning flashed through the sky, and the thunder grew louder and more ominous. Within a few minutes, a raging storm had enveloped the entire lake. It rained so hard that no one could see the warriors, even during bright flashes of lightning.

As hail pelted the camp, the women and children retreated into their tents. Around them, trees snapped and branches tore holes in the tipis. Grandparents huddled together, and women and children cried with fear.

The wind and rain blew all night long. When the storm finally passed and the sun came up, everyone ran through the debris and down to the lake.

A few feet from shore, the warriors' shattered boats drifted toward them, with bits of hair and feathers clinging to the sides.

Owanda stood sadly with his people.

"We desecrated the lake with our hatred," he said. "Now it has avenged itself."

The Song of Howastena

History offers one other explanation for Devils Lake's haunting name, with a story that describes mysterious cries of the lost and the damned, echoing across a deserted isle. In the late 1800s, a Dakota man named Howastena shared this account with Jerome Hunt, a Catholic missionary. Oddly enough, while he described the voices of the doomed, Howastena's own name meant "Beautiful Voice."

HOWASTENA WAS BORN in 1863, on a peninsula on the west side of Devils Lake, near the modern-day town of Minnewaukan. When the water was high, the peninsula became an island. Cut off from the rest of the shoreline, it also became a haven for ghosts and spirits.

"One night in summer," Howastena said, "when there was no moonlight and darkness was so thick that the island could not be seen from the mainland, strange sounds were heard. The beating of a drum came across the water, the sound of chanting and confused voices mingled with the usual rustle of leaves and swish of waves.

"There was great wonder in the camp. Could Chippewas have come so close? Could friends be looking for us?

"In the early dawn a number of Dakotas swam over to the island and searched the woods. But a few frightened deer and small animals were all they found.

"So real had been the sound of voices in the night, and so regular the beating of the drum, that they could not believe the sounds to have been made by winds or animals.

"From that time they called the lake *Mini-wakan,* or Holy Lake. What you call the Devil's Heart we call the Heart of the Holy Lake."

The sounds Howastena described are still audible to this very day. They haven't changed over the century that has passed; the beat of drums still echo through the trees, and the low murmur of voices still drives some passers-by to distraction.

The History of Devils Lake

Before you meet more of the ghosts of Devils Lake, let me tell you a little about the area.

You probably wouldn't come across the area by accident. It's in northeast North Dakota, close to the Canadian border, in a place that even residents will admit sometimes feels like the middle of nowhere. Except for die-hard hunters and fishing enthusiasts, outsiders almost never venture into the region. Just getting there feels like a pilgrimage—whether you drive across hundreds of miles of open prairie, take an overnight train from Minneapolis, or fly in on one of the small commuter planes that connect to larger hubs.

Once you do manage to arrive, however, you can't miss the lake itself. It's enormous. It stretches out in every direction, with coves, arms, and bays that twist across the landscape as far as the eye can see. The water covers more than three hundred square miles.

TO THE ANCIENT Dakota people, Devils Lake was a holy place. It was carved by an ice-age glacier twelve thousand years ago, and its waters were filled with magic and mystery.

The Indians called it "Mine-wakan"—Spirit Lake. A mistranslation, however, led to the ominous, sinister name—and a quirk of punctuation omitted the apostrophe that would claim the lake as the devil's own.

To the traders, trappers, and travelers that came from Europe and Canada, the lake was a dark and dangerous location. The entire region was wild and untamed, and explorers soon realized that their survival in the area was never assured. Most moved on as quickly as they could.

In 1863, when President Lincoln opened the Dakotas for settlement, a few hardy pioneers plowed their way into the territory. In the 1880s, as the railroad tycoon James J. Hill forged the Empire Line, thousands more came by train—all hoping to build their own empires of freedom and prosperity.

Most were immigrants from Norway and Germany. Everyone jostled for land, power, and a new life that none of them could have dreamed of back in the old country.

The men came first. They built lean-tos, shanties, and sod huts. They bought seed with credit and plowed their claims with borrowed tools. They planted trees and set down roots. Then they sent for their wives and children, and put them to work, too.

For the most part, the land they found around Devils Lake seemed to be waiting just for them. The soil was easily converted from grassland to cropland; it was a blank slate for development and dream building.

But the prairie wasn't uninhabited, as they first assumed. In fact, the Lake Region was already filled with the stories of the Dakota people. The natives followed the buffalo herds across the prairie and lived in movable villages of tipis, pulled by horses, strong women, and constantly shifting tribal affiliations. It was also the domain of French Canadian Voyageurs, who combed the countryside with dogsleds, because they knew that the land boasted some of the richest hunting, fishing, and fur-trapping in the world. And it was home to the loud, lusty, larger-than-life *Métis*, the inevitable result of the cross-cultural exchanges that unfolded when the fur trappers married Native American women and started wilderness families of their own. The Métis followed the buffalo, too, in a cacophonous caravan of ox carts, with squeaky wheels that could be heard for miles. In fact, if you stand quietly enough, you can still hear them, far away on the horizon.

Today, about seven thousand people live in the City of Devils Lake. It's the seat of Ramsey County, so the courthouse is there, along with a hospital and a community college. Devils Lake is also the center of the Lake Region area, made up of several adjoining counties: Cavalier County to the north, Walsh County to the east, Nelson County to the southeast, Benson County to the southwest, and Towner County to the northwest.

Summers are hot, winters are cold, and most of the area looks just as it did a hundred years ago. In fact, many of the same buildings still stand. From the outside, they look just like they did at the turn of the last century. You can even see old-fashioned painted murals and advertisements on the brick walls—each one a faint reminder of the past.

If you ever find yourself in Devils Lake, it won't be hard for you to imagine yourself traveling back in time. Step into the old Great Northern train station, and you can still hear the murmured voices of all the travelers who came before you. Walk the city streets, and you'll sense the hustle and bustle of a booming pioneer town. You can catch fleeting glimpses of women in long dresses, and men on horseback. Stand on the wind-swept prairie, and you'll spot ghostly farmers plowing their fields with steam-powered tractors, and teams of hired men harvesting the crops. And if you visit the reservation, on the southern shores of the lake, you can still catch a glimpse of ghostly Dakota Indians, striding through sun and shadow.

The Museum Ghost

Lillian Wineman might be the most famous ghost in Devils Lake. Before she died, she was an eccentric old woman who shouted through her door whenever anyone who came to see her. The rest of the time, she lived alone in a house filled with antiques and Indian artifacts. After she died, her belongings were moved to the Lake Region Historical Center—and she moved there with them.

LILLIAN WINEMAN WAS a misfit. As the only child of a wealthy Jewish merchant, she didn't mesh well with the Protestant and Lutheran children who surrounded her. As an adult, she didn't really fit in with the other women of the town, either. She never married, and she never had children. Instead, she developed an affinity for the Dakota Indians just south of Devils Lake—and while she became an inveterate collector of their artifacts and handmade crafts, she was forever destined to be an outsider, looking in on a culture even more foreign than her own.

Lillian was born in 1888, in a house on the corner of Sixth Street and Third Avenue. She had curly red hair, wide-set eyes, and a pointed little chin.

Her father, Sam Wineman, owned a clothing store on Main Street, on the corner of Fourth Street and Fourth Avenue—and from the moment Lillian was born, Sam swore that his only child would have everything her heart desired.

When Lillian wanted a doll to play with, he gave her two. When she wanted a toy tea set, he imported a set from Europe, handcrafted of translucent porcelain with hand-painted flowers. He even bought her a pony. Sadly, she cried when she saw the horse he chose for her. Its red coat matched her hair, and she was afraid people would laugh when she rode it.

Lillian didn't drink milk like the other children in town. She drank cream, as she would for the rest of her ninety-five years.

Lillian didn't play with the other children, either. Not only were the other children poor, but most of them were Scandinavian or German.

Lillian didn't fit in.

Lillian Wineman as a young girl

By the time she was a teenager, Lillian's parents sent her to a private boarding school in Minnesota, so she could take finishing lessons with a higher class of girls.

Lillian spent most of her life in Devils Lake. After finishing high school hundreds of miles away, she came back to Devils Lake to graduate with the class of 1906. The senior class photo from that year shows her seated stiffly on a curtained stage, with fourteen other girls and four young men. Every one of them is wearing a white shirt with a starched collar and tie. The boys have black jackets, and the girls have long skirts. Not one of them is smiling.

After she graduated, Lillian continued to live with her parents, where her father continued to shower her with increasingly elaborate gifts. He bought her a one-cylinder Cadillac, for example—but when he realized the car couldn't make it up the hill to their summer house by the lake, he hired a crew of men and machines to cut the hill down.

Mr. Wineman also decided to make a place for his daughter by turning his store into a cultural center for the community. He turned the second floor of the business into a five-hundred seat opera house, complete with a grand staircase and bay windows overlooking Main Street.

The theater helped people forget, just for a night, that they had stationed themselves in a hostile wilderness with interminable winters and impossibly hot summers. For a few hours at a time, they could imagine that they were in Chicago, or New York, or London, enjoying a performance of Shakespeare.

The Devils Lake High School class of 1906. Lillian is in the first row, second from the left.

Lillian and her mother dressed up for events at the opera house. They bought most of their clothes in Minneapolis, four hundred miles to the east. Lillian favored satin dresses with trains, suits with brocaded trim, and embroidered silk shawls. She accessorized her eveningwear with ostrich-feather hats and long kid gloves.

Not content to host traveling shows, Mr. Wineman also sponsored a community theater group, to ensure that Lillian would have her own place in the spotlight. Before long, Lillian became one of its star players.

By all accounts, she was actually a talented performer. When someone offered Lillian an audition in New York, however, Mr. Wineman refused to let her go—and he disbanded the little theater group.

In fact, Lillian's father refused to let her work for as long as he lived.

Instead, Lillian and her mother spent winters in Los Angeles and summers at Chautauqua, an annual festival that featured lectures, plays, and concerts on the shores of Devils Lake.

Every year, Native Americans would come from all over North and South Dakota to perform at Chautauqua. Lillian would watch them dance—and then she would bargain with them for their arts and crafts. Her father, after all, had money, and Lillian had never been denied anything she wanted.

Eventually, she collected enough ceremonial clothing, war clubs, peace pipes, and beadwork to fill the front room of her house. In her later years, she told a newspaper reporter that Native Americans had fascinated her since she was ten years old. She was convinced that they had been cheated by history.

"We don't even own the land we live on today," she said. "It was stolen from the Indian by the white man moving west."

The Indian artifacts were especially precious to her, she said, because so few people recognized their value during her lifetime. When she held them, she could see the people who created them. She treasured their history, and she preserved it as best she could.

When her parents died, Lillian also inherited everything they owned, including a pair of oversized mahogany statues carved by prisoners in England in the fifteenth century. She inherited her mother's silver, cut glassware, and hand-painted china. Her father left her a library of antique books with the complete works of Charles Dickens, a Bible that was nine inches thick, and a leather-bound history of North Dakota from 1910. She also inherited their imported, high-end furniture, including a divan and overstuffed chairs, with carved lion's heads carved into the arms.

She moved it all into a little cottage near the Chautauqua grounds. She hung two stern-looking portraits of her parents on the wall, and for the rest of her life, they watched her every move.

Lillian never married. She never had children, and since she had been an only child, she never had nieces or nephews, either. When visitors came to see her, she would answer the door with a challenge. "Who are you," she'd shout, "and what do you want?"

The Wineman fortune eventually ran out, so Lillian found ways to support herself. During World War II, she worked as a riveter at Douglas Aircraft in Los Angeles. For a time, she worked for the Devils Lake Chamber of Commerce. She also clerked in local hardware stores, and she even drove a taxi.

In her spare time, Lillian was a writer—although she would laugh aloud when her friends called her that. She usually wrote stories and poems about the things she loved: Chautauqua, her childhood, her memories of Devils Lake and North Dakota history. Her work was never published.

A few months before she died, Lillian's friend Eleanor Wilcox decided to write a newspaper article about her. She asked her if she would have changed anything about her life.

"Everything," Lillian said.

Lillian's Wineman's life ended quietly. She died as she had lived—essentially alone, comforted by her favorite possessions.

When she reached her nineties, a broken hip had forced her into a nursing home. Her neighbors closed up her house, but they brought her a trunk filled with her Indian beadwork. In her small room at the nursing home, she would sort through it all with a far-away look in her eyes.

Lillian's nursing home bills put her into debt, and when she died in 1983 almost everything she owned became the property of the state of North Dakota.

In 1986, her belongings were moved into the old post office building on Fourth Street, just a block east of her father's clothing store and opera house.

Almost immediately, strange things started to happen—and the staff began to suspect that Lillian had moved into the museum, along with her things. Lights on the second floor on and off by themselves. Visitors and staff members hear footsteps when they know they're the only living souls in the building. Painters and maintenance men who work after hours sometimes hear someone whistling in their ears, and passers-by report loud music inside after midnight. Some people have seen a woman standing in the doorways and looking out windows, late at night when the museum is closed.

Lillian seems to have a special affinity for babies and very young children, who look up and gurgle and coo as if they're being entertained by an amusing adult.

In Room 201, however, children who try to touch Lillian's things feel an invisible hand on their arms, pulling them back.

Officer Sneesby's Last Patrol

Lillian Wineman isn't the only ghost at the old post office. She's often joined on her rounds by a police officer named Charles Sneesby, who was gunned down in the alley on a moonless night in 1924.

ON A TUESDAY night in June, 1924, two young men driving past the Devils Lake Post Office at midnight spotted Officer Charles Sneesby lying on his back in the driveway, arms outstretched, illuminated by the light of his own flashlight. There was a bullet hole between his eyes.

Sneesby's attackers were a gang of four would-be burglars—or "yeggs," in local slang. Sneesby, the town's night watchman, had the misfortune of running into the gang's lookout just as the burglary was getting underway. The lookout panicked and fired his .38. The policeman never knew what hit him.

The four yeggs ran to their car, which they had parked, ironically, in front of the hospital where Sneesby would die moments later. Two men were sitting on a porch near the post office, and they saw the gang run past, carrying the suitcases they had planned to fill with stolen loot. The thugs piled into a 1923 Big Six Studebaker touring car and raced out of town. And even though the sheriff sent men to close all the roads, they were too late.

The thieves, police pointed out, were bunglers—not career criminals. The *Devils Lake World* described their mistakes. "There were four men in the gang, and they could have easily overpowered the officer and gagged him had they any desire to do so," one report read. "This is always the habit of professional criminals, who only shoot in order to save their own lives."

They had cased the building, and they knew that the last postal worker left for home at midnight. That's when they pried a screen off a window, jimmied it open, and sneaked inside.

What the thieves hadn't figured out, however, was that there was no money to be had in the post office safe. At the end of every business day, a clerk took all the receipts to the bank. What would they have found in store? Little more than a stack of one-cent stamps.

A vintage postcard featuring the Devils Lake Post Office

Investigators recovered the acetylene and oxygen tanks the burglars had set up to cut the steel door of the post office vault, but it took them another ten years to find Sneesby's killer—a thug named Goldie Nolan, who eventually was the first North Dakota criminal to be sentenced to life in California's Alcatraz prison.

Sneesby, 53, had only been a police officer for a year. He was a semi-retired contractor who had lived in Devils Lake for twenty-one years.

Sadly, if Sneesby had taken his police dog on his rounds that night, he probably would have lived. He usually patrolled with an Airedale that ran ahead of him and barked. On that fateful night, however, he left the dog at the police station.

Almost a hundred years later, people still catch glimpses of Officer Sneesby on patrol—especially on warm summer evenings, when the sun sets late over the northern plains and dusk stretches long into the night. That's when people see a shadowy figure moving slowly around the building, following a ghostly beam of light. Sometimes they even hear the echoing sound of a dog's bark, and they know that Officer Sneesby's four-legged partner has finally joined him on his rounds.

The Lightman at the Opera House

You don't have to venture far from Lillian Wineman to find another ghost from her era. Just walk two blocks west, to the corner of Fourth Street and Fourth Avenue, where the Wineman Opera House still stands. While it hasn't housed a production for many, many years, at least one of its crewmembers is still working backstage.

FOR A FEW short years, the Wineman Opera house was a hub for entertainers. Lillian herself performed there with her friends in the O'Callaghan Troupe. A photo in the Historical Center shows the actors in costume, ready to stage *A Midsummer Night's Dream*.

Local performers weren't the only ones who trod the boards, either. Touring productions from New York frequently made their way through the small-town theaters of North Dakota. Al Jolson had his first starring role at the Grand Theater in Fargo. Boris Karloff spent a year at the Jacobson Opera House in Minot. Traveling vaudevillians brought burlesque, and politicians took to the stage to give speeches during campaigns.

The auditorium could accommodate five hundred people, and audiences dressed up for every performance. The town's merchants wore three-piece suits with waistcoats and bowler hats, while their wives wore evening gowns and long silk gloves. Farmers wore black coats and homespun dungarees. Occasionally, even Dakota Indians from Fort Totten would make their way into the audience, along with rowdy mixed-blood Métis, who lived for singing, dancing, and celebration.

After each show, the men would help the women into their wraps and fur coats. They'd climb into their horse-drawn carriages and wagons and return to their homes, where their children slept, and then trundle off to bed themselves.

One man, however, rarely left the Opera House.

His name has been lost to history, but most people didn't know it when he was alive, either. Everyone just called him the Lightman.

At the turn of the last century, electricity was a rarity—especially on the prairie. Theater stages were illuminated by gas lanterns and clean-burning kerosene lamps, and footlights were essentially open torches.

It was the Lightman's job to ensure that the fires stayed under control, because no one ever wanted to yell fire in a crowded theater.

In Devils Lake, the Lightman seemed old, even when the city was young. He was bald, and he wore a long white beard like Father Time. He walked with a shuffle and his wrinkled hands shook, so it usually took him a while to get all of the lamps burning and adjusted before each performance. And while he was present for every show, he didn't waste his time enjoying the entertainment. All of his energy was focused on the lights. He would watch intently for a telltale spark, or the popping sound that suggested a light was getting too hot. When he needed to adjust the lights, he would creep through the shadows to change them. Because he knew where the lamps cast their light, he knew where the corresponding shadows fell, and most audiences never even knew he was there.

After each show, he would wait for the last man in the audience to leave, and then he would see the performers out the door. With measured movements, he would turn off every lamp and extinguish every fire—except for one. He would leave a single lantern lit for himself, so that he could leave the building, too.

When Sam Wineman announced that the Opera House would be closing, the Lightman only nodded. He understood. Moving pictures were growing in popularity. Touring theater productions were slowing down. The opera had had its moment in the sun, and it was time to move on.

The last show played to a packed house—and when the last beautiful woman on stage had sung her last note, the audience rose to its feet to give the old theater a rousing goodbye.

That night, the Lightman turned out the lights for the last time. It wasn't long before his life faded into darkness, too.

But the Lightman never really left the second floor of the Wineman building, which has long since been converted into apartments. Today, the people who live there can hear him shuffling through the halls and corridors. When light bulbs need replacing, he flickers them in warning first. And when they leave lights on at night, he turns them off.

The Maiden on the Cliff

While we usually think of cowboys and Indians going head to head in the Wild West, Native Americans also fought among themselves for control of Devils Lake. As the population grew in the Midwest, the Ojibwe people pushed the Dakota people out of Minnesota, forcing them into the Lake Region. When the Chippewa tried to follow, the Dakota pushed them back.

At some point during the 1800s, a group of Dakota fighters captured a young Ojibwe boy—the son of a chief—and used him as a human shield. We'll call the boy Migizi, the Ojibwe word for eagle.

People in the Devils Lake region used to think this story was a legend. Eventually, however, a turn-of-the-century hunter discovered two men who could verify the tale from beyond the grave.

MIGIZI WAS ONLY ten when the Dakota warriors kidnapped him. Even so, he never let them see his fear. He did what he had to do to survive—and he survived by pretending to become one of the Dakota.

Eventually, his captors believed he had lost interest in his own people. As he grew from a child to a man, they gave him more and more freedom in their camp. They even trained him to fight. Someday, they hoped that he would go into battle against his own father.

It was a sordid scheme, but Migizi was too smart for them. Secretly, Migizi had devised the perfect escape—one that would bring him both freedom and happiness.

His plan grew over time, as he grew to know Winona, the Ojibwe chief's first-born daughter. That's what her name meant, in fact: first born. She had a heart-shaped face, smooth skin, and sparkling brown eyes. She had a dusting of freckles across her nose, and she always wore a mother-of-pearl necklace.

Winona also had a soft heart. When her father's men first kidnapped the young Migizi, she felt sorry for him. They were the same age, and Winona tried to put herself in his place. Winona couldn't imagine being taken from her family the way Migizi had been torn from his tribe. To assuage her own sense of guilt, she would often sneak across the camp to talk to him, in the darkness, when everyone else was asleep.

An Indian woman photographed in 1910 by Edward S. Curtis, and a young Sioux man photographed in 1899

Over the years, over many nights of whispered conversations, Winona and Migizi grew closer, until they fell in love.

The young couple knew that they could never be together as long as they stayed with the camp. For one thing, Migizi had never forgotten his own people, the Ojibwe. But more importantly, Winona's father had promised her to another man—a young Dakota warrior named Zica.

On the night that Winona's wedding was announced, she and Migizi decided to escape.

They packed a few meager possessions: a hunting knife, a string of beads, and some pemmican to eat. They wouldn't need much for their journey, Migizi assured her. Once they reached his home, they would be reunited with his family. His parents would bless their marriage and give the young couple everything they needed.

They didn't count on Zica, however. The jilted warrior loved Winona and hated Migizi. When he discovered that the couple was missing, he set out to bring Winona back to the camp—alone.

Zica found the young couple on a hill near Medicine Lake. The moon was almost full that night, and the two young men could see each other clearly.

Both were tall and slim, with coiled muscles and quick reflexes. They had trained together with the older warriors. They knew the same moves, and they knew them well.

For a single moment, as the young men faced each other on the hillside, neither one moved. Then they pulled their knives. A glimmer of moonlight glinted off the blades, and the two men lunged at each other.

Migizi stabbed his attacker in the stomach. The young warrior clutched his side, dropped to his knees, cried a death song to the sky, and collapsed.

Migizi, meanwhile, stood with his hand on his neck. When he looked at Winona, his eyes were open wide. She rushed to him and pulled his hand away to see the damage for herself.

It was just a small cut, on the left side of his neck. As soon as she moved his hand, however, blood began to surge from the open wound with every beat of his heart.

"It's only a scratch," Winona assured him, but they both knew better. Migizi slumped to the ground, and Winona cradled Migizi's head in her lap until his body grew cold. Then she curled her body around his. She lay next to him for hours, until she too fell asleep.

While she slept, she dreamed that Migizi was calling to her from the hills near Mini-wakan, the holy lake several miles to the north.

"I have traveled to another world," he told her, "but I'm not too far ahead of you."

He reached out and started to show her visions of the life that waited for them, if she could reach him in time. She saw him standing in a wooden lodge, complete with a stone fireplace and a bed of soft buffalo robes. She saw him hunting in the woods, and fishing in Mini-wakan's clear blue waters. She saw herself picking wild berries in the meadows near their home.

Migizi also promised that he would give her two children—a boy and a girl—and that he would tell stories to them every night.

"Our children will grow up strong and healthy," he told her, "but we will never grow old. If you hurry, you can join me here. Please try to catch up. I'll wait for you as long as I can."

Winona woke up and wiped the tears from her eyes. She smoothed her bloodstained dress and headed north toward Mini-waken.

She walked for miles, determined to reach Migizi before sunset. She seemed to glide across the prairie—almost as if she were already a ghost herself.

As she climbed the high bluffs overlooking the south shore of the lake, she sang love songs and pictured Migizi smiling and urging her on.

She reached the crest of the hills just as the full moon started to rise.

It was the biggest full moon she had ever seen. It seemed to fill half the sky, and its light silhouetted her slender form.

Winona raised her arms high, as if she was greeting someone in a deep embrace—and then she tumbled over the cliff and into the waters of the lake two hundred feet below.

To this day, on the night of the harvest moon, Winona's spirit returns to the hillside. Some people see her dive headfirst into the shimmering water. She looks virginal, young and beautiful, draped in soft veils of light. Others hear her love songs echoing from the bluffs, like chanted poetry, and look up to see her shining like a star, rising into the Spirit World.

For years, newcomers to the area thought the legend was a myth, but that changed on October 27, 1900, when a settler named J. M. Mulvey found the skeletons of two men on a hill near Medicine Lake. They lay as if they had fallen in battle, in remnants of native dress … and each one had a knife by his side.

The Ghost Wife

If you've never been on the prairie at night, the miles of open space can be overwhelming. In the darkness, the earth disappears, and the skies seem to grow even larger in proportion. You can see stars, millions of them, stretching out above and around you in every direction. If it weren't for a small radius of ground at your feet, you'd think you were floating in space.

From that perspective, it's easy to see why people throughout history could picture the souls of the dead at home in the stars. The ghost wife in this story is one of them. According to native legend, she not only found her own place in the heavens, but she also took her family there to keep her company.

TOMAHAWK AND SPOTTED Bird were a young married couple, and they were very much in love. They had two daughters and a third child on the way, and life was good. Shortly after Spotted Bird gave birth to their third daughter, however, she died.

Tomahawk was so distraught he couldn't talk. He chopped off the little finger of his left hand to show his grief, and he cut off all his hair. He stopped eating and spent all of his time staring into the fire.

His mother, a hunch-backed old woman, had to move in with him to take care of the new baby and two older girls. One day, some of the old woman's friends stopped by, and Tomahawk overheard them talking about a path to the spirit world.

Tomahawk snapped to attention.

"Where is this path?" he demanded.

"It's near Mini-wakan," one of the elders said. "The path begins in a passageway, in the corridor between two hills."

Now, there is actually is a corridor between two hills near Devils Lake. The hills are called the Devil's Ears, and you'll find them on Highway 57, on the way to Devil's Heart—a local landmark you'll hear about later.

For as long as anyone can remember, that corridor has been a travel route. Before the highway was built, it was an Indian trail. According to legend, travelers would lose their mind while they traveled between the hills, but they would regain their sanity when they came out on the other side.

A Dakota medicine man, photographed in 1907 by Edward S. Curtis.

Even now, there are people who refuse to drive along that stretch at night, because they've seen horrible demons on the side of the road—demons who manage to chase their cars without moving, and who appear and reappear along the road as if they're standing still.

"It's a very dangerous place," one of the old women told Tomahawk. "Once you step into that corridor, your mind will snap. Most people don't come back. Those who do return are changed forever. It's as though they leave a piece of themselves behind."

At that moment, Tomahawk decided that he would find the passageway, because he knew his wife would be waiting for him there.

He hugged his mother and thanked her for her help. He kissed each one of his three daughters, filled a leather pouch with pemmican and dried berries, and left for Mini-wakan that same day. Before long, he reached the two hills the elders had described.

Near the base of the hills, he spotted an old man sitting on a bear rug, in front of a tipi that was covered with stars. The old man seemed to know why Tomahawk was there.

"You don't look dead to me," the old man said.

He was right. Tomahawk only looked half-dead.

"I have to find my wife," Tomahawk replied. "I don't care about anything else."

"In that case," the old man said, "I can help you. The passageway is only for spirits, but I can show you how to leave your body here. I'll watch over your physical form until you return."

The two men smoked a pipe together, and then the old man taught Tomahawk a magic spell that would allow him to step out of his body.

Tomahawk lay down on a striped blanket in the grass. He felt a tingling sensation, and then realized that he was looking at himself lying motionless on the ground.

The old man looked straight at his spirit form and motioned toward the hills. "Go on," he said. "Go quickly. Go find your wife."

The corridor between the hills was dark and shadowy, and it echoed with the sighs and moans of the dead. Tomahawk couldn't see anyone else, but he could hear their breathing, and he could feel spirits brush past him.

The passageway was cold and damp, and Tomahawk shivered. Even in spirit form, he could feel sharp pebbles underneath his feet, and thorns and brambles scratched his spirit legs.

He gathered his courage and pressed ahead.

Before long, Tomahawk realized that he was walking through a heavy fog. He continued walking until he saw his wife coming toward him, through the mist.

She seemed angry.

"Where are the children?" she asked him. "How could you leave them? You're not supposed to be here!"

"I'm not dead," he said. "I haven't left them forever. I just had to see you one more time."

Spotted Bird listened as Tomahawk described his journey to the two hills.

"You know," Spotted Bird said, "the Spirit World isn't so bad. If you like, I could arrange for you and the children to join me. We could travel to the Milky Way, and we could be a family again."

The thought of arranging for his children's death shocked Tomahawk back to reality.

"I'm not ready to die, and I don't want our children to die, either. Can't you come back and live with us?"

Spotted Bird said she would find out.

"Go wait for me at the guardian's tipi," she said. "I'll meet you there in three days."

Tomahawk retraced his steps and slipped back into his body, where the old man chanted and helped him back to life with a potion of brewed roots and leafy herbs.

Together they waited for the next three days. The medicine man seemed unconcerned. He played a flute and watched the clouds roll by. Every now and then, he seemed to say something as a bird or an insect flew past, but Tomahawk could never make out the words. He was too distracted to wonder what the old man was saying, anyway. He spent most of his time pacing and looking toward the two hills.

"Sit down," the old man warned him, chuckling. "You'll scare the spirits."

At midnight on the third night, a thick fog enveloped the tipi. Just as she had promised, Spotted Bird appeared. She looked like a misty, half-formed gauze, and Tomahawk could see right through her.

"It's all set," she said. "I'm allowed to come back to life. I just have to spend three nights in the shaman's tipi, and then you and I can return to the children. While I'm inside, though, you can't look at me or try to talk to me. If you do, I'll be sent back to the Spirit World—so don't try to look, and don't breathe a word to me."

Tomahawk couldn't have looked if he had wanted to. The guardian had put a spell on him so he couldn't move. For three days, he sat on the striped blanket outside the tent, happy with the knowledge that his wife was a few feet away.

Tomahawk could hear the guardian in the tipi with her. He could hear him chanting and singing, and he could smell the pungent herbs and grasses he burned in a fire. Every now and then, the walls of the tent would lift up and out, as if a strong wind was circling inside.

After three days, the tent flaps parted and Spotted Bird stepped out. She was no longer a spirit; she was strong and healthy, and as beautiful as she had been when Tomahawk first married her.

Together, they returned to their village. Tomahawk's mother was able to retire with her friends, and Spotted Bird was able to care for her three children.

After a while, however, Tomahawk seemed to forget all he had gone through to regain his wife. He started to take her for granted. He didn't thank her for the meals she cooked, and he didn't compliment her care of the children. He even decided he would like a second wife in his tent, and he married another woman.

"It will be great," he told Spotted Bird. "You'll have someone to help you with your work, and you'll have a friend to keep you company when I'm hunting or fishing."

Spotted Bird didn't share his enthusiasm for Tomahawk's new wife. The woman he had chosen was younger and prettier than Spotted Bird, which was bad enough—but she was vain and selfish, too. She didn't do her share of the work, and she criticized Spotted Bird's cooking and worse, her children.

Both women went to Tomahawk with their complaints about the other, but he laughed them off.

"You women will have to work this out amongst yourselves," he said, and he walked off to track some animals down by the lake.

One night after supper, the new wife turned to Spotted Bird in a rage.

"Why are you even here?" she asked. "You're not a real woman. You're a ghost. You belong in the Milky Way, not down here on earth. You should have stayed dead."

Spotted Bird didn't say a word to the new wife. She called her children into the tipi and tucked them into bed for the night. Tomahawk sighed and followed them in. It was summertime, so the new wife pulled a buffalo robe outside and slept under the stars.

The next morning, however, when she went into the tipi to get something to eat, she discovered that the tent was empty. There was no sign of Tomahawk, or Spotted Bird, or the children. There was no trace of Tomahawk's hunting or fishing gear, or their cooking equipment, or the children's toys. There weren't even any footprints in the tent; the grass stood tall and unbent, as if no one had ever stepped inside.

Spotted Bird and her family had disappeared without a trace. She had taken them all to the Spirit World overnight, rather than stay with the new wife down on earth.

After that, no one else wanted to live with the new wife, either. They thought she was cursed, and she was doomed to live out her days alone in the empty tent.

The Haunting of Mary Berri Chapman

One woman in Devils Lake came to terms with a ghost wife of another sort. She found herself becoming friends with her husband's first wife—even though she happened to be dead.

MARY BERRI CHAPMAN was a writer and painter from Washington, D. C. She was beautiful, smart, and talented—and in 1897, when she married a handsome senator from North Dakota, she climbed to the top of the Washington social scene.

At the time, Mary was just twenty five years old—but she had already earned fame as a promising young author. Her first book of poetry, *Lyrics of Love and Nature*, had just been released, and *Harper's Magazine* had published one of her short stories.

In photos, the young woman's beauty is striking—even by contemporary standards. She seems serene and thoughtful, with inquisitive dark eyes and porcelain skin.

Her husband, Senator Hansbrough, was a much older forty nine. Before he had been elected to political office, he was a newspaper man who had learned the trade in California. In 1881, he went to Dakota Territory, where he parlayed his media prominence into a political career. He was the first representative from North Dakota in 1889, and he became a U. S. Senator in 1891.

The first Mrs. Hansbrough, Josephine, had passed away during a long, cold winter a few years before. She was only forty two, but she was cut down by a raging infection in the days before antibiotics could have saved her.

After her death, newspaper reports described her as a woman of rare grace.

"She was most devoted to her husband, and a true friend," one journalist wrote. "She treated all with whom she came in contact in her daily life with kindness and consideration. Whether carrying flowers to some sick child in her North Dakota home, or sustaining the dignity of her State at the National Capital, she was the same generous, sweet-spirited, loving woman."

Both houses of the North Dakota Legislature adjourned when she died. They drafted resolutions of respect, and held a joint memorial session. It was the first time in the history of the United States that any legislature met to pay a tribute to the memory of a woman.

Mary Berri Chapman, photographed by Frances Benjamin Johnston (1898)

Little did they know that she wasn't truly gone.

Even though the marriage was the first for Mary Berri Chapman, the wedding ceremony was surprisingly low-key.

"There were no bridesmaids, best man, or ushers," *The New York Times* reported. "The bride was given away by her mother. She was dressed in a gown of corn-colored silk with brocaded stripe and trimmed with ruchings of tulle. She wore a white leghorn hat, trimmed with plumes."

When Mary Berri Chapman moved into her new husband's house in Devils Lake, his first wife's presence was everywhere.

Josephine had decorated the home in the style of the day, with a formal armchair and a settee in the parlor, and a small table in the entryway.

For all her fame and public acclaim, Mary was still a young and inexperienced woman, and she wasn't brave enough to redecorate completely. Instead, she started with small touches, like a new vase on the mantle, and a new bedspread in their bedroom.

For the most part, the senator hardly seemed to notice her changes. He smiled politely when she pointed them out, and then went back to his reading.

When Mary suggested that they get rid of Josephine's bentwood rocker, however, the senator put his foot down. It was a comfortable chair, he said. It looked good by the fireplace. He liked it, and it would stay.

No one ever sat in it, though. And at night, when she and the senator were both in bed, Mary could swear she heard it rocking back and forth.

Her husband's first wedding photo bothered her, too. She moved it to a back room, but someone kept moving it back to the front of the house. While Hansbrough swore he never touched it, eventually Mary gave up and left it on display. After all, the newlyweds spent most of their time in Washington, in a home that Josephine had never seen.

Even so, it seemed as though Josephine remained a presence in their lives together.

Before her marriage to Senator Hansbrough, Mary Berri Chapman had written stories and poems that bordered on the maudlin. After her marriage, her work became even more macabre. It almost seemed as though she were writing poems for her husband's first wife.

Consider this poem, which was published in 1906.

A MESSAGE

I am still here, who died.
Still am I at your side,
In earth and heaven—see
The elements of me!

*In every flower's face
My likeness you can trace.
In every voice you hear
A note I spoke once clear;
In all my like, that grows,
That flashes, flutters, glows.
To sight, taste, hearing, touch,
In all I loved so much,
I live—nay, do not start—
I live within your heart!
Do you not feel me here.
Who died—but am still near?*

As time passed, Mary seemed to grow more comfortable with the ever-present memory of her husband's first wife. Life with a senator could be lonely. North Dakota seemed like an empty place, especially when Henry was away on business. Eventually, she even came to think of Josephine as a friend.

RESURRECTION

*To-day a rose, to-morrow withered bloom!
Grieve not, fair flower, at your early doom.
Immortal in my memory's garden close
I'll resurrect your lovely spirit, rose.
You shall not die, nor ever hope to rise
And live again,—I'll be your Paradise!*

When the senator's second term ended in 1909, he and Mary Berri Chapman moved back to Devils Lake. They lived there peacefully, ghosts and all. Mary turned from writing to painting: one of her portraits, painted of a Dakota man, is now in the collection of the Library of Congress.

After ten years, the Hansbroughs retired to Florida. When the senator died in 1933, they were living in Washington, D. C. again. His remains were cremated and surreptitiously scattered under an elm tree at the capital—but no one in Devils Lake knows what happened to Mary Berri Chapman.

The can only speculate that she died as she had lived, comforted by the ghost of a woman she had never met.

Duncan Graham's Island

There was a time when everyone in Devils Lake knew Captain Duncan Graham, the first white settler in the Devils Lake region. These days, he's probably not someone you want to meet—especially after dark.

DUNCAN GRAHAM WAS a fur trader. He stomped when he walked, wore a beard to shield his face from the cold, and talked with a thick Scottish brogue.

At the age of twenty, he had left everything but his accent in Scotland and headed to North America. He made his way to Hudson's Bay in Manitoba, and from there he traveled south into Dakota Territory, to set up his own trading posts in the Red River Valley.

The War of 1812 brought his trading days to a temporary halt. Graham was a British subject, so he joined the British army and fought against the United States. At the time, both nations were battling for control of the Northwest Territories.

Graham was a war hero. He helped take Prairie du Chien from the Americans in Wisconsin—and in the process, he drove his opponent down the Mississippi River. His opponent just happened to be Zachary Taylor, who would go on to become president of the United States.

When the war ended, Graham headed west again. He traveled to Devils Lake in 1815, settled on the lakeshore, and built a trading post. For three years, he traded with the Native Americans, who would bring in animal furs in exchange for blankets, beads, knives, and kettles.

It should have been a peaceful, idyllic existence—but it was anything but serene.

Graham's wife, Susanne Istagiwin Hazahotawin, was a prominent Dakota woman he had met in Minnesota. She was part French, but she was also the daughter of an Indian chief.

Mixed marriages are rarely easy, and the Grahams had their share of cultural clashes. In fact, Duncan Graham's Native American in-laws called him "Hoarse Voice"—probably because he grumbled and yelled so much.

Graham almost reached his breaking point in 1818. At that time, Native Americans didn't bury their dead. Instead, they built burial scaffolds high above the ground, so the bodies would be out of the reach of animals.

Unfortunately, for Graham, one of those scaffolds was built near his home—and mourners gathered at the site for weeks on end.

Graham described the scene in a letter to John Allen, surgeon of the Royal Navy.

"There was continually, night and day, somebody crying or howling over these bones. He was father to one, brother to another, and cousin to a third, and so on. In short, where he had one relation in his life, he had 500 after his death. They *are* related together, as they originated from the devil, whom I think must be the great-grandfather of them all.

"This has been the most disagreeable winter that ever I passed in my life. I have experienced more trouble, anxiety and danger since the 18th of October than in the whole course of my life before. I wouldn't undergo as much again for all the beaver that went out of Hudson's Bay in ten years. I am in hopes to go straight to heaven as I have every reason to think that I have already gone through purgatory. I have given the place where I am the name of hell upon earth, as I can find no other name more becoming it."

Eventually, that long, noisy winter came to an end, and Graham left his trading post in Dakota Territory to continue his military career. Along the way, he switched sides and became an American citizen. He was commissioned as a captain in the U. S. Army, and he was stationed at Fort Snelling, Minnesota. During his time there, he helped broker a peace agreement between two warring factions—the Dakota people and the Ojibwe.

He died near Fort Snelling on December 5, 1847. After he died, a part of him returned to his former home on Devils Lake, in search of the peaceful existence that had evaded him during life.

Today that island is a state park, named in his honor. Grahams Island—which is actually a peninsula on the northern shore of the lake—is one of the best places to fish in America. It's covered with oaks, elms, box elder, poplar, and cottonwood trees. For a nominal fee, campers and other visitors can access a boat ramp, a bait shop, a campground, and cabins.

Looking over their shoulders, however, is a shadowy figure who peers out from the woods that cover the land—just as it did a hundred and fifty years ago, when Captain Graham first settled there.

Given the hard life he led and the number of years he's been dead, it's not surprising to learn that he's a tired old man, a shadow of his former self. His shoulders are stooped and his posture is guarded, but his eyes open and alert.

For the most part, he's a calm, non-threatening presence, content to hike the territory that bears his name. In the thick undergrowth of the wooded peninsula, he wanders—in sunshine by day, and at night by the light of the stars. If you look closely enough, you can even find the trees where he marks the monthly cycles of the moon and the changing of the seasons. If you do happen to catch a glimpse of him, you'll probably notice that he seems to float about a foot off the ground.

Duncan Graham loves winters, because that's when his island is quiet. He also loves the snow, because he doesn't feel the cold anymore.

Noise, however, drives him crazy—especially after dark, on summer nights when the campground is full. Every year, a few families have to leave in the middle of the night with their frightened children in tow.

He gives most offenders a warning. If you're making too much noise, he'll probably blow a cold wind down the back of your neck. He might drop sticks and branches on your tent, or send sparks from your campfire shooting past your head. You could even sense him standing behind or beside you—but when you turn to see him, he'll disappear into a mist or fade away, like the flickering light of a firefly.

If you continue to cause a commotion, the penalties increase: he'll send biting ants, stinging bees, and mosquitoes into your tent. He might even materialize: an angry, bearded Scotsman, with fiery eyes and menacing fists.

And you'll hear his raspy voice, still with a thick Scottish brogue, commanding you to quiet down—or be chased off Duncan Graham's Island altogether.

The Resurrection of Little Flower

The tale of Little Flower's death and resurrection is one of the spookiest stories of all time. This account first came to us from Marie McLaughlin, Duncan Graham's granddaughter, in 1916. Her husband James was a government agent at Fort Totten, on the shores of Devils Lake, from 1871 to 1881.

LONG AGO, WHEN the Dakota Indians were the only ones who lived in Dakota Territory, a man and a woman had a daughter, late in life. She was their only child, and they loved her with all their hearts.

They called her Little Flower, and she was just as sweet and beautiful as her name. By the time she was a teenager, all the young men of the tribe wanted her for a wife. One by one, they tried to convince her to marry them, but she always said no.

One cold, wet day, Little Flower came down with a cold. Before long, her cold turned into pneumonia. Her parents tried every remedy they could think of, and they called in all the best medicine men and women, but nothing could cure Little Flower. As her parents held her in their arms, she died.

The whole village grieved. All of the elders said she had been like a daughter to them, and all of the young men felt as though they had lost their best chance for happiness.

They wrapped her body in soft robes and blankets, and they carried her to a scaffold several miles from the village. That was their custom: they built a framework of four posts, and then they made a bed of willows across the top, seven feet off the ground. They believed that Little Flower's soul would have an easier time reaching heaven if she were closer to the sky.

Little Flower's parents underwent the tribe's other traditional mourning rituals, too. After her funeral, they gave away their finest belongings. They cut their hair short and dressed in plain, simple clothing. And though it almost killed them to do so, they even gave away all of Little Flower's things, because didn't want her spirit to feel earthbound by her possessions.

After a year had passed, the old couple's friends tried to convince them to end their mourning period.

Karl Bodmer, "Funeral Scaffold of a Sioux Chief near Fort Pierre" (1844)

"It's been long enough," they said. "You're both old, and you should make the most of the time you have left. You should try to enjoy whatever pleasures life has to offer."

The old couple could only shake their heads and say, "We have nothing to live for. Nothing in this world could ever have any meaning for us. When we lost our daughter, we lost the light of our lives."

They continued to mourn, and another year went by.

One evening, a hunter and his wife happened to walk past the scaffold that held Little Flower's body. They were returning from a hunting expedition, dragging heavy travois sleds that were loaded with wild game.

There was a spring about a half mile from the scaffold, where a clear stream of water created a little oasis of sweet green grass. That's where the hunter and his wife decided to camp for the night. They tethered their horses and put up the small tipi they used when they were traveling.

The hunter's wife had just built a fire in center of the tipi and started to cook dinner, when their dogs started growling and barking at something outside.

"Go see what they're barking at," the hunter told his wife.

She ducked out through the small flap of the doorway and then rushed back in.

"There's someone walking toward us," she said. "I think it's a woman, coming from the direction of the scaffold."

Within a few minutes, they heard soft footsteps outside the tent. The hunter and his wife could see a small pair of moccasins at the door.

In the calmest voice he could manage, the hunter said, "Whoever you are, please join us and have something to eat."

Without a word, the figure came into the tent and sat down. Her head was covered with a robe, and a soft blanket was drawn tightly over her face.

The hunter's wife filled a plate with venison and boiled turnips. She put it in front of the visitor and said, "Eat, my friend. You must be hungry."

The figure didn't move.

"Let's give our guest some privacy," the hunter said, "so she can enjoy her meal in peace."

The wife turned around and made herself busy, separating the meat and the sinew from the backs of the deer they had killed. The hunter filled his pipe, turned away from the door, and smoked in silence. After a few minutes, they heard the figure push her empty dish across the floor. Without looking at the visitor, the hunter's wife picked it up, cleaned it, and put it away.

The robed figure didn't seem to be moving at all. She didn't make a sound, and she wasn't breathing.

After a few minutes, the hunter said, "Are you Little Flower, the girl we placed on that scaffold two years ago?"

The figure bowed her head two or three times, in a long, slow nodding motion.

"Would you like to sleep here tonight?" he asked. "We can make a bed for you."

The figure shook her head no.

The hunter took a long, slow puff from his pipe, and asked, "Will you come see us again tomorrow?"

The figure nodded yes.

For the next three nights, Little Flower visited their tent, never saying a word, and never making a sound. She ate the meals they gave her, and then disappeared into the darkness.

On the third night, however, the hunter noticed that Little Flower was breathing. He also saw one of her hands protruding from the robe. Her skin was black and leathery, and it had shriveled into the bones of her hand.

The hunter was an ordinary man with an extraordinary gift for healing. He stood up and reached for a medicine sack that hung on a pole. He took out some roots and mixed them with skunk oil and vermillion. "If you'll let me put this medicine on your skin," he said, "I think it will rejuvenate your hands."

The figure held out her hands, and the hunter rubbed the medicine into her skin. She nodded in thanks and left.

The next day the hunter and his wife moved their camp closer to their home village. When night came, their dogs started barking again. The hunter's wife looked out and saw that the girl had followed them to their new location.

She came into the tent and sat down. This time, the hunter noticed that the girl's robe seemed looser, especially over her face—and when she reached out to take her supper, her hands looked healthy and normal.

"It looks like the medicine helped you," the hunter said.

The girl nodded yes.

"Would you like enough for the rest of your body?"

Again, she nodded.

"I'll mix it," he said, "and then I'll go outside and let my wife help you put it on."

After a few minutes, the job was done, and the hunter's wife called him back into the tent.

"Tomorrow," he said, "my wife and I will go back to our village. Do you want to come with us?"

The figure shook her head no.

"Will you come visit us there?"

She nodded her head yes.

"Will you want to see your parents?" he asked.

She nodded again, stood up, and walked off into the night.

The hunter and his wife traveled back home. As soon as they reached their village, they went to see Little Flower's parents.

The old couple could hardly believe the news of their daughter's resurrection. They followed the hunter and his wife back to their tent, and at sunset they all sat down together to wait for her.

As usual, the dogs started barking outside.

"She's coming," the hunter said. "She probably doesn't look the way you remember her, so you'll have to be brave. Just take a deep breath. In a minute, you'll see your daughter again."

Right at that moment, Little Flower stepped into the tent. She had cast off her blankets and robes, and she was dressed in a soft leather gown. She looked as healthy and beautiful as she had before she died.

Her parents began to weep. For the next several hours, they hugged her close and smothered her with kisses, while Little Flower told them about her life in the Spirit World, where she had spent two years drifting around the Milky Way.

"I don't know what brought me back," she said. "I just remember hearing the hunter and his wife talking as they walked past my scaffold. It seemed as though I was simply waking up from a long sleep."

The old couple wanted Little Flower to return home with them that night—but she had another idea.

"I don't think I can," she said. "I want to stay with the man who gave me a second chance at life."

After a brief discussion, the hunter agreed to take Little Flower as his second wife. His first wife didn't mind; she had always liked Little Flower, and since she had witnessed her ordeal, she thought of the girl as a sister. They all got along well, and over the next few years, the hunter shared his gift for healing with both of them. Eventually, however, the hunter was called to join a war party, and he was killed in battle.

A year after the hunter's death, Little Flower married again—but her second husband was killed, too, by a band of horse thieves. She took a third husband, and he was killed in a hunting accident.

At that point, all of the men in the village feared Little Flower. They said she was holy, and that anyone who married her would die before his time.

Little Flower moved back in with the hunter's first wife. Together, the two women cared for the sick and injured people in their community. Eventually, Little Flower became known as one of the most skillful healers in the nation. They both lived to a ripe old age, treating the sick and breathing new life into people who were at death's door.

At last, when Little Flower was a very old woman herself, she felt death approaching her once more. She asked her lifelong friend, the hunter's wife, to take her to the scaffold where she had rested once before. Together, the two old women hobbled across the prairie. With her friend's help, Little Flower crawled to the top of the scaffold. She wrapped herself in blankets and robes, laid flat on her back, and took her last breaths.

Just before she closed her eyes, she turned to her friend.

"This time," she whispered, "I'm here to stay."

Yellowstone Vic

In his day, Yellowstone Vic was one of the most famous characters in the northern territories. His name is mostly lost to history now, but for a time he was just as well known as Buffalo Bill or Calamity Jane. He worked as a hunting guide for Theodore Roosevelt, capitalizing on his reputation as a champion buffalo hunter.

YELLOWSTONE VIC WAS actually Grant Smith, born in 1850 near Buffalo, New York. His parents moved west, but at the age of thirteen, he ran away from his family's home near Alexandria, Minnesota. By seventeen, he was carrying mail between Fort Totten and Grand Forks, as well as Fort Abercrombie near present-day Fargo.

At the time, the settlement in Grand Forks was only a wolf station—a shelter for hunters who killed wolves for a living. The outdoorsmen sold the pelts and earned a bounty for every tail, so during the fall and winter they could earn a decent living.

One fall, when the air was frozen and the ground was covered with frost, a rich prospector named Brown arrived at the wolf station. He told the men he had five thousand dollars in cash, and he needed a safe place to keep it while he was in camp.

One of the men, however, was a shady character named Robinson. He had been there for a month, lounging around and irritating the others.

The wealthy Mr. Brown had been with them for three days when the shifty Robinson suddenly announced that he was going to Fort Abercrombie. He left without much fanfare.

Meanwhile, young Yellowstone Vic was on his way toward Grand Forks—and he had the bad fortune of meeting the devious Robinson on the trail.

"Hello, Vic," Robinson said. "That's a nice horse you're riding."

Yellowstone Vic agreed—but he couldn't help noticing that Robinson's horse was even better.

When Robinson suggested that they trade, Vic thought he was getting a deal—especially when the stranger offered to throw in fifty dollars to sweeten the bargain. Just before they parted ways, Robinson also handed Vic a pistol, and told him to put it in his saddlebag.

At seventeen, young Vic didn't realize that he had just been set up for a crime he didn't commit.

Vic was feeling good when he pulled into the next dog station on the trail. He fixed himself a supper of bacon and bread, and he had just finished eating when a six wolf hunters stormed through the door.

They didn't say anything at first. "If you want any supper," Vic told them, "you can help yourselves. There's plenty of bacon and flour."

The six men roared with laughter. "You've got considerable gall, youngster," one man said, and then they dragged him out of the shanty. They bound him hand and foot, and then they drove a stake into the ground and tied him to it. They left him there to freeze overnight, while they went inside to have supper.

Vic shouted. He screamed. He begged them to untie him. None of the wolf hunters would reply. Instead, they all turned in and slept through the night.

The next morning, they found Vic numb and frozen stiff, but not dead yet. He was covered in frost, and he was barely breathing. His hands and feet were swollen to twice their normal size from the hemp they had tied tightly around his wrists and ankles. One man loosened the bonds, but the rest declared that they should hang him immediately.

Yellowstone Vic still didn't know why he was being punished.

"You're riding a dead man's horse," the men told him. "He was killed on the trail, murdered in cold blood, all his money gone."

The scurrilous Robinson, after all, had known that Mr. Brown would be leaving the wolf shack. He merely got a little ahead of him on the trail, and then he waited. When Mr. Brown passed by the next day, he murdered him. Another traveler found the body, informed the wolf men at the station, and the six hunters set off in search of frontier justice.

Yellowstone Vic begged them to go to Fort Totten to check his story. He had been there just two days earlier; there was no way he could have killed a man further along the trail.

Most of the men didn't want to bother, but one of them heard a strange voice whisper in his ear.

"This is not your man," the whisper said. "This is not your man."

The hunter looked around for the source of the voice. He couldn't see anyone but his associates and the poor, suffering Vic, half dead with cold and exhaustion.

"This is not your man," the voice said again, even more firmly than before. "This is not your man."

The hunter convinced the rest that they should give Vic a chance. He saddled his horse and rode to the fort while the rest of them waited for the verdict.

When he returned with confirmation of Vic's story, the hunters let him go—and Vic went on to became one of the west's most vocal critics of vigilante justice.

Little Crow and the Indian Uprising

Most people remember that Abraham Lincoln led the nation through the Civil War between the North and South. Few realize that the country was also fighting a second civil war, between white settlers and their Indian predecessors along the western frontier. In fact, the battles in America's new territories were worse than anyone back east could have imagined.

AS THE NATION expanded in the 1870s and '80s, most Native Americans were forced to trade their lands for a subsistence-level lifestyle. It wasn't a fair exchange—and it was made worse by the fact that those who were entrusted with the Indians' annual payments were shifty and corrupt. When the Indians would report to the country's military outposts for their annual twenty-five dollar payments, the government agents—surrounded by soldiers, contractors, and merchants—would cheat them, insisting that the Indians somehow owed most of their allotment for the meager services and provisions they'd already been given. Without representatives or advocates of their own, most Indians would go home to their hungry families, empty-handed and ashamed.

In August 1862, a group of tribal leaders asked government agent Tom Galbraith to distribute a warehouse full of provisions to their starving people. Andrew Myrick, the trading post operator, responded with venom.

"So far as I'm concerned, if they are hungry, let them eat grass or their own dung."

Until then, most of the Indians had seemed placid and controlled. Suddenly, they snapped, and hundreds of repressed warriors went on a bloody rampage.

They attacked every white settler they could find. They killed the men, quickly and brutally, with guns, arrows, axes, and tomahawks. The murders were surprising, but understandable, even to government representatives of the time.

What happened next, however, horrified the rest of the country. Once the men were dead, the Indians tortured their defenseless wives and children. They cut off women's hands and feet. They disemboweled them as they screamed for mercy. They roasted infants alive in their mothers' ovens, and impaled small children on spikes, leaving them to die in their fathers' abandoned fields.

Little Crow

The insurrection went on for weeks. The Indians killed at least seven hundred people; some estimates put the number at a thousand. Another thirty thousand pioneers ran for their lives.

White settlers were spread out across hundreds of miles of open countryside. Most didn't have advance warning of the rampage. A few were able to flee to scattered forts and trading posts, but there weren't enough soldiers on hand to move out into the countryside and rescue the families that were still under attack. It took days for word of the revolt to get back to Washington D. C., and weeks to send troops west to take the land back from the Indians.

Because the Indians had nothing, they thought they had nothing to lose. They couldn't have been more wrong. By the time the cavalry arrived, in fact, the Indians had done just about all the damage they could do, both to the white settlers and to their own reputations.

Chief Little Crow was asleep in bed when a group of Indian men came to tell him that a war had begun.

For years, he had tried to persuade his people not to fight. He was smart, sophisticated, and media savvy. He charmed reporters in Minnesota and Washington, D. C. with his wit and subtle use of sarcasm. He knew the futility of trying to subdue the dominant culture.

That night, as an angry mob surrounded him in his home, he almost talked them out of their aggression. His followers were ready to surrender peacefully and let the insurrection die.

But in a desperate last maneuver, one man called Little Crow a coward. Fully awakened, Little Crow replied, "I am not a coward. I will die with you."

Little Crow inherited his name from his grandfather, who always wore the skin of a crow over his chest. He was the fourth generation of men in his family to become a tribal chief—but his father had bestowed the honor reluctantly. His other son, Little Crow's brother, had died in battle. When Little Crow's father realized that he was going to die, too, he told Little Crow that he didn't have any other choice but to name him the new chief—and he gave him some advice.

"Be honest," he told him. "Make yourself respected by the white people. It's a shame that you have very little good sense."

Little Crow tried to adapt to a new way of life. He went to Washington to meet with federal officials. He dressed in white European clothing, joined an Episcopal church, built a house, and started to farm.

After the uprising, Little Crow knew that his efforts had been meaningless. He stopped wearing western clothing, and he went on the run, a fugitive.

Stunned by the violence on the western frontier, newspapers and everyday Americans decided that the only good Indian was a dead Indian. Spurred on by popular anger, the military was determined to crush the insurgence—and to destroy any chance the Indians had to rise up ever again.

The Army marched, and hundreds of Native Americans were captured. Thirty-eight of them were hanged in Mankato, Minnesota, in a mass public execution that still outrages modern-day activists.

Thousands more, however, were able to evade the Army. As the troops moved in from the east, four thousand Indians moved west to their ancient hunting grounds in the Dakotas, near the sheltered coves and bays of Devils Lake.

For a time, it almost seemed as though the Indians had a fighting chance. Their escape to Devils Lake, however, would prove to be just a temporary reprieve; the mere fact that the Indians were fleeing made them guilty in the eyes of the military.

When Generals Henry Sibley and Alfred Sully marched toward Devils Lake in 1863, they were especially anxious to capture Chief Little Crow. He managed to evade them, and he returned to Minnesota.

A few days later, on July 3, 1863, a farmer named Nathon Lampson and his young son Chauncy spotted Little Crow and his son Wowinapa near Hutchinson, forty eight miles north of New Ulm. Little Crow and his son were picking berries, and they didn't notice the Lampsons. Lampson leveled his rifle and fired. Little Crow was hit, but not killed.

Little Crow returned fire, striking the elder Lampson in the shoulder. Lampson fell to the ground, gravely wounded. Lampson's son Chauncy fired at Little Crow, killing him. Then Chauncy ran towards Hutchinson, where several soldiers were camped. They all raced back to the scene of the firefight.

In the meantime, Little Crow's son fled on horseback, and the wounded Lampson regained consciousness and stumbled into Hutchinson under his own power.

The cavalry found Little Crow's dead body. They scalped him and cut off his head. Oddly enough, they didn't realize they were dealing with Little Crow—even though they should have recognized him. After all, his description was well known: he was of medium height, he was between fifty and sixty years old, and he had gray hair. His right arm had once been broken and hadn't been set correctly, and his left arm had withered. Most tellingly of all, however, he had an odd double row of teeth in his mouth, both front and back.

After the soldiers mutilated Little Crow's body, they brought it to Hutchinson and threw it into a slaughterhouse cesspool. Little Crow's severed head lay on the prairie for several days until someone picked it up and put it in a showcase.

From prison, Wowinapa described his father's death. The second shot had killed him, he said, but not instantly. "I'm a dead man," he told his son. Then he asked for a sip of water, and died.

At the time, the white people saw a certain irony in Little Crow's death. Many relished the fact that a young boy had killed the old warrior—especially in light of the fact that Little Crow and his men had killed so many young boys and their fathers. The settlers also liked knowing that his body had been mistreated, in retaliation for the hundreds of victims who lay on the prairies for weeks before they could be buried.

The young Lampson received five hundred dollars for killing Little Crow. In 1868, a janitor donated Little Crow's scalp to the Minnesota Historical Society. In 1896, a farmer donated the skull. Others had donated some of the bones. Eventually, in 1971, historians returned Little Crow's remains to his descendants for burial.

In Devils Lake, however, some people still notice Little Crow's presence. He's spotted occasionally in the trees, walking slowly, and peering over his shoulder at something no one else can see.

They notice, too, that whenever there's trouble between Native Americans and white people—a bar fight, or an outbreak of racism—someone leaves crow feathers in those very same trees.

It's as though Little Crow can't rest until relations between the two sides are back in balance.

Alfred Sully's Game of Chance

For three years, General Alfred E. Sully and his men maintained a presence near Devils Lake. Every summer, they camped on a hill almost three hundred feet above the lake. A few years later, that hill would be named in his honor. From the top of the hill, it's still possible to watch over the people Sully used to guard—but now the tables have turned.

ALFRED SULLY NEVER thought of himself as a gambling man. That's because he believed in being prepared for every possibility, and he calculated all of his decisions wisely.

After the Indian Uprising of 1862, the U. S. government was determined to control the Dakota Indians on its western frontier. In 1863, two generals were sent after thousands of Indians who had fled west: Henry Sibley, a former Minnesota governor who controlled the state militia, and Sully, who had earned a reputation as an Indian fighter in other parts of the west.

Sibley was supposed to drive the Indians west toward the Missouri River, and Sully was supposed to head up the Missouri and intercept them before they could cross the river into the western part of Dakota Territory.

Sully started immediately for Sioux Falls, so he could march his men to the scene. When he got there, however, he discovered that his men weren't assembled, the supplies weren't in store, and his support ships couldn't make it up the drought-choked river. He started out anyway, trusting that his provisions would catch up—but when he learned that the delay had cost his colleagues the battle, he prepared an alternate response, by planning an attack that would define his entire military career.

Meanwhile, as Sully was still struggling to move his men north, his counterpart Sibley had defeated the Dakotas in three battles: at Big Mound on July 24, Dead Buffalo Lake on July 26, and at Stony lake on July 28. The Indians didn't suffer many casualties, though—so when Sully didn't show up to carry out his end of the mission, the whole plan collapsed. The Indians were able to cross the Missouri River and escape the Army's grasp completely.

Alfred Sully

General Sibley had no way to follow them, so he turned around and headed back to Minnesota. Sully, who never did manage to get his expedition completely underway, reached the scene a month later.

From the safety of western Dakota, the Indians had seen Sibley and his men retreat. Their scouts followed them all the way into Minnesota, so the Dakota people thought they were in the clear. They crossed back across the Missouri river and resumed their buffalo hunt in the east.

On September 3, an advance contingent of Sully's men found the Indians in camp at White Stone Hill, twelve miles west of the present town of Ellendale, North Dakota.

Three thousand Indians were camped at the site. Some of them were the same people that General Sibley had driven across the Missouri River a month before, but most of them were newcomers who had joined the group out west. They were truly Dakota Indians. Most of them had been in Dakota Territory for years, and they'd had nothing to do with the Indian Uprising in Minnesota.

A thousand Indian warriors surrounded Sully's advance men. For a while, the isolated soldiers thought they would be slaughtered.

The Dakota chief, however, wasn't in a hurry. He believed that his captives were as good as dead, and he wanted to make an occasion of their demise. He ordered his warriors to hold off with their executions until necessary preparations could be made. The women began to cook a celebration feast while the men covered themselves in war paint.

It took all afternoon for the Indians to get ready for battle—but just when they were about to charge, in the cool of the evening, General Sully and the cavalry rode into sight.

The Indians were outnumbered. Within minutes, the Indians were in full retreat. The men stood to fight while the women and children ran for their lives—but in less than an hour, Sully and his soldiers had killed every warrior in the camp. Then they went after the fleeing women and children, and killed hundreds of them, too. The next day, Sully's men destroyed the tipis, bedding, and provisions the Indians had left behind.

Sully prided himself on his thoughtfully executed plan. Just to make sure that it would stick, he returned every summer for the next three years, marching north with his soldiers across the land, rounding up any Indians he encountered, and shuttling them all to reservations and forts.

At the end of each march, he and his men would camp on the side of Sully's Hill. While they were there, they would relax with cards and a few bottles of whisky.

A year after they packed up and left for the last time, Fort Totten was established nearby, and other soldiers moved in to the area to build a sawmill, stockade, artillery magazine, blacksmith's shop, and quarters for eating and sleeping.

Something strange started to happen on the high slope above them, however. The men at Fort Totten could never escape the feeling that they were being watched by invisible sentries on Sully's Hill.

The young soldiers would drink to dull the constant sense of unease they felt at the site, and they would play cards to break the boredom—but then they would start to fight amongst themselves.

More than one man stormed out of the card games, only to freeze to death in winter's unforgiving cold. The next day, their comrades would find them buried in ice and snow, just a few yards from the fort's perimeter walls.

Some men lost everything they owned in their all-night games of poker and dice. They continued to drink, however, and fritter away their remaining Army pay in hopeless games of chance.

There are those who say the young soldiers were the victims of a curse: a marvelous curse executed from beyond the mass graves Sully left in his wake. While the Indians he had killed couldn't beat Sully and his men at their own game, they did manage to turn the rules of the game against them.

There's a certain irony in the fact that today, Sully's Hill overlooks the Spirit Lake Casino, a multi-million-dollar hotel, restaurant, and resort complex that provides jobs for hundreds of Indians from the Spirit Lake Nation.

Haunted Fort Totten

Fort Totten was the first permanent settlement near Devils Lake. Today, it's a state historic site. Step through its gates, and you can stroll wooden boardwalks and explore a series of brick buildings that date back to the 1870s. You can shop for souvenirs in the gift store, or window shop in Plummer's store—a re-creation of an old-time trading post. You can tour the Pioneer Daughter's Museum, or see a Broadway musical in the Fort Totten Little Theatre. You can even stay overnight in the original officers' quarters, which have been turned into a period-style bed and breakfast.

And if you're a ghost, you can walk through the walls.

FORT TOTTEN WAS haunted from the very first day of its existence. The site, after all, was named for a dead man—Joseph Gilbert Totten, an Army general who had passed away a year before.

Originally, the fort was just a crude collection of log cabins on the south side of Devils Lake. Pierre Bottineau, a celebrity Métis guide who rose to fame during the mid-1800s, led General Alfred Terry to the site in 1867, and Terry brought in machinery for a sawmill. By winter, he and a ragtag band of infantrymen had constructed an artillery magazine, a blacksmith shop, stables, and living quarters. They all settled in behind an eighteen-foot oak stockade.

The first men stationed at the fort were foot soldiers. The U. S. government had sent them to defend the border between Dakota Territory and the British possessions of modern-day Canada. The soldiers were also supposed to protect the territory's mail route, and defend any wagon trains that passed through the area on the way from southern Minnesota to the gold fields of Montana.

The men passed their time on patrol, drilling for maneuvers in the ongoing Indian Wars, shooting at targets, and hunting wild game in the woods. They also planted gardens in the spring.

The Northwest Fur Company sent an agent to the post, assuming that he would be appointed as the fort's official trader. Instead, General Terry appointed a man named E. W. Brenner to fill the position.

An early view of Fort Totten

Brenner didn't waste any time. He built a store southeast of the fort—and he put together a brewery, where he could brew ten barrels of beer in a week. The soldiers at the fort were a captive market, and Brenner was a local hero.

Two years later, Congress approved construction of a newer, better post, just a few hundred yards south of the original fort. The soldiers abandoned their temporary log shelters for brick buildings—most of which still stand.

A number of famous men passed through the fort in its early years. Major Joseph Nelson Garland Whistler was stationed there in 1868; he was related to James McNeill Whistler, the artist who painted his iconic mother. In 1887, Captain Frank Baldwin reported for duty. He was one of only nineteen Americans in history to be awarded two Congressional Medals of Honor. General William T. Sherman, the Civil War hero, visited after the war. He even cruised Devils Lake on the steamboat *Lillie Lee*, which had been built by Fort Totten soldiers.

The most famous person associated with the fort, however, was Sitting Bull. He staged his first attack on the U. S. government there, and he organized his warriors to raid mail carriers and military horse herds throughout the 1860s and 70s. The Army major he met there, James McLaughlin, would ultimately bring him down in South Dakota.

A lot of men, women, and children have lived within Fort Totten's walls—and many of them have never left. You'll get to know them better in the next few pages.

The Ghost of Pierre Bottineau

It's safe to say that Fort Totten and the City of Devils Lake wouldn't have come into being without Pierre Bottineau—the handsome, larger-than-life frontiersman who single-handedly founded dozens of settlements across the upper Midwest. Today he still travels the ancient trails he first explored as a boy.

PIERRE BOTTINEAU. For people in North Dakota and Minnesota, the name comes tripping off the tongue, just as it has for a hundred and fifty years.

Pierre Bottineau was six feet tall, with copper skin and chiseled features, and his dark eyes twinkled whenever people gathered around him. He had a lust for life—and love, as evidenced by the twenty-three children he fathered. He was the first person to lead Army surveyors to the shores of Devils Lake, as they laid the groundwork for a fort that would defend a westward-growing nation. He had a knack for knowing which hunting and fishing camps would be ripe for settlement—so along the way, he also claimed large tracts of prime acreage for himself, selling it later for a fortune.

He negotiated treaties between the U. S. government and the native tribes, because he spoke at least six languages—and because he knew how to throw great parties that could bring opposing factions together. Some people called him "The Walking Peace Pipe."

Pierre Bottineau was born on New Year's Day, 1817, in a hunting camp not far from Devils Lake. His father was a French Canadian, and his mother was an Indian. He used his charm and his mixed Métis heritage to make the best of both worlds.

As a boy, he traveled with his father, a Voyageur who earned a living as a hunter, trapper, and fisherman. As a young man, he also drove caravans of ox carts, moving people and their possessions across the Canadian border, through Dakota Territory, to and from the commercial settlements on Minnesota's Mississippi River.

In the winter of 1837, Bottineau was guiding three men through the North Country when they were caught in a ferocious blizzard. Two of the men died in the cold. Bottineau and his surviving companion pushed on for twenty-six days without seeing another living soul. Eventually, they were forced to kill and eat their dog, before they reached a trading settlement.

Pierre Bottineau

By the 1850s he was a celebrity adventure guide, leading wealthy tourists on hunting trips through the new frontier. In 1853, he led the first preliminary survey ever made for the Northern Pacific Railway.

In 1862, he happened to be in Dakota Territory when the Sioux Uprising began. Some of the Indians attacked Fort Abercrombie, where Bottineau was staying. He slipped out under cover of darkness and headed for Sauk Center, so the U. S. Army could respond. After that, he scouted for General Sibley's military expedition into North Dakota.

Eventually, Bottineau grew old and retired to northern Minnesota, near his birthplace. At that point, the United States Congress voted to give him an almost-unprecedented pension of fifty dollars a month. He stayed active: he sat on the village council of Red Lake Falls from 1882 to 1887, and he was its president in 1885. He even helped negotiate a final land treaty with the Pembina Ojibwe in 1889.

Bottineau passed away in 1895, at the age of seventy-eight. Some say he died as he had lived, on a moose hunt near Thief River Falls.

That doesn't explain, though, why he's still sighted in the land where he grew up.

You can see him late at night, especially in the fall, when the nights get cold, the leaves change color, and there's a hint of frost in the air. He appears as a faint mist, rising up from the ground and slowly taking human form.

He's usually alone—although occasionally, he'll be accompanied by a young boy or girl, the spirit of one of his children. He looks about thirty-five: perpetually young, and preternaturally healthy. He wears an old, outdated suit and a long cloth coat, and he typically walks down the middle of the road. Drivers don't see him until it's too late, and then they drive right through him, leaving him unharmed.

It seems nothing can harm him—in life, or in death. If that strikes you as strange, consider the fact: while all those around him suffered and died, Pierre Bottineau himself escaped death a thousand times.

Some credit his years in Devils Lake with his ability to outsmart death. Others wonder if there's a more sinister explanation. Did Pierre Bottineau outwit the devil himself in order to continue hunting, trapping, and fishing until the end of time? He was a champion negotiator, after all. He spoke a multitude of languages.

Perhaps, on that fateful trip through snow and storms in the winter of 1837, Pierre Bottineau met the devil in a vortex of swirling snow. As he stared into the void, the devil challenged him to live his life as boldly and bravely as he could—and Pierre Bottineau rose to the challenge, and won.

The Story of Brave Bear

Ghosts want their stories told. Like the rest of us, they want their lives to be remembered, and they want their accomplishments to be admired. That's true even when their achievements don't seem all that commendable.

One of the most interesting characters in the long and storied past of Devils Lake was Brave Bear, a fugitive who vowed to destroy the men who brought him to justice. In the end, he did get his revenge—but only from beyond the grave.

BRAVE BEAR WAS an outlaw, a Dakota man who lied, cheated, and stole from anyone he could as he traveled back and forth through Dakota Territory. George Faribault and James McLaughlin were his lifelong adversaries—two government agents who tried to keep him in line, even when they couldn't keep him in jail.

Brave Bear and Faribault first met in 1873, on a dirt road near Fort Totten. At the time, Faribault was the head of farming at the Devils Lake Indian Agency, and it was his job to ensure that the people there had enough to eat. He was trying to teach the Indians how to farm, because the government wanted Native Americans to settle on reservations and open the rest of their land up to white settlers.

On the day they met, Brave Bear was passing through the area with some of his friends.

"I haven't seen you around here before," Faribault said.

"No," Brave Bear replied. "We're from Standing Rock. We're visiting."

Something about Brave Bear's attitude spelled trouble. Maybe it was the way he seemed to gauge everyone he met. Like a grizzly, he was a natural predator who could size people up, calculate their value to him, and measure what type of opponent—or prey—they'd be in a fight.

There was also something unnerving about the look in Brave Bear's eyes. Most people have a spark of light in their eyes—a reflection of something hopeful and bright—but when Faribault looked into Brave Bear's eyes, it was like staring into a piece of black obsidian.

"Well," George told him, "be sure to stop by the fort for some provisions. We'll give you enough to eat while you're here, and a little extra to take home."

Brave Bear

The next day, Brave Bear and his men did visit Faribault, and he gave them the food he had promised. Four or five days later, they stopped back again, and he gave them provisions for their journey home.

But instead of going south, as they had said, they headed north to the Canadian border. That's where they decided to rob a family of settlers—and when the men fought back, he killed them.

Brave Bear traveled on. A year and a half later, he and his men returned to Devils Lake. This time, they had been joined by Brave Bear's brother, Isnakiyapi, or "The Only One." And this time, they decided to settle in for a while.

Nobody at fort Totten liked the Brave Bear gang. They were aggressive. They drank. They fought. They threatened the other Dakota men, and they leered at the women.

When Faribault learned that Brave Bear and The Only One had also been accused of murder, he teamed with Army Major James McLaughlin to arrest them and send them east for trial.

George Faribault and a Wisconsin Indian named John Grass, in a photo by David F. Barry

Brave Bear and his friend didn't go quietly. Surrounded by soldiers at the fort, Brave Bear tried to jump out of a second-floor window. Dragged outside, The Only One dropped his blanket, dropped low to the ground, and sprang away from the soldiers who had been holding him.

He sprinted around Faribault's house, with the soldiers running behind him, firing. One of the shots hit him in the leg. Injured, he turned and faced a sergeant with his knife drawn, like a wild animal at bay—but the sergeant fired and The Only One dropped to the ground, shot through the heart.

Brave Bear looked at his dead brother and surrendered without a fight.

The soldiers took Brave Bear to the guardhouse on the fort. After a few days, he was carted off to a jail in Fargo. From there, he was moved to a jail in Pembina, the scene of his crime, where he would be tried.

He spent his time in jail watching his guards carefully, quietly learning their policies and procedures. He spotted their weaknesses—and he escaped.

Almost inexplicably, he made his way back to Fort Totten.

James McLaughlin

The other Dakota people reported his reappearance, but before the Army could arrest him again, he slipped away. He headed south for his old home at Standing Rock—but he was a fugitive, a wanted man with the Cavalry in hot pursuit, so he wasn't safe there, either.

Brave Bear decided to make his way west toward the Red Cloud Agency in Nebraska. Just a few days into his trip, he ran into a soldier near Fort Sully. He killed the man and took his rifle, his clothing, and a thousand dollars in cold, hard cash. The money, which would be worth about thirty thousand dollars today, made Brave Bear feel even braver. He decided to head back to Devils Lake with the cash.

When he arrived, he found an uncle and gave him forty dollars. During his visit with his uncle, though, a policeman's wife spotted him and ran to tell her husband. The policeman gathered reinforcements and headed out to arrest Brave Bear. Along the way, they ran into Brave Bear's uncle, who was heading to the trading post to spend some of the money. The policeman told the old man that they were looking for Brave Bear, so Brave Bear's uncle doubled back through the woods to warn him that the police were on the way.

Immediately, Brave Bear crafted a plan to ensure that he could escape without being pursued. When the police arrived, he told them that three thousand hostile Indians were on their way to kill everyone at the agency—and that he had only come to warn them of the onslaught that was headed their way.

Sitting Bull

The troops were put on alert. Their commanders ordered the soldiers to resist the attack and save the fort. All the Indians came in from the agency and offered their services to help. Guards were stationed everywhere, watching and waiting for the enemy to approach.

Of course, there was no enemy in the area—but in all the commotion, Brave Bear slipped through the woods into Canada.

For a time, it seemed as though Brave Bear had outsmarted the frontier legal system, and that he would get away with his crimes. His life certainly took a turn for the better.

Once he was in British Possessions, he joined Sitting Bull's band. He even married one of Sitting Bull's daughters. After all, he had plenty of money. He could afford to pay for the safety of a new life, with a wife and a distinguished father-in-law.

But something in him just couldn't leave the thought of Fort Totten alone. He wanted revenge.

He tried to get a half-dozen Indians to join him and head back to Devils Lake. He wanted to kill Major McLaughlin and George Faribault, because they had arranged for his arrest in the first place—and they had turned him into a fugitive.

He planned to go back to Devils Lake and knock on Faribault's door in the middle of the night. When George Faribault opened the door, Brave Bear planned to shoot him dead—and then he planned to travel to Major McLaughlin's house and kill him, too.

Brave Bear couldn't convince anyone from Sitting Bull's tribe to accompany him, though. Eventually, Brave Bear put his plans for revenge on hold. When Sitting Bull and his band traveled to Standing Rock, Brave Bear traveled with them.

Brave Bear put his plan back into motion when he learned that Major McLaughlin would soon be joining them in South Dakota. McLaughlin had been promoted, and in 1881, he was on his way to his new post as head of the Standing Rock agency. What's more, George Faribault had also been moved to the Indian Agency in Sioux Falls.

Ultimately, however, Brave Bear wasn't prepared for a confrontation. He panicked. He actually drew attention to himself when he tried to swim across the Missouri River to escape. He was captured by some settlers on the scene, and they brought him to the nearest U. S. marshal. It didn't take long for the marshal to put the story together—and justice eventually caught up with the once-fearless outlaw.

Brave Bear was sent on to Yankton, South Dakota, where he was tried for the Pembina murders, along with his escapes and his plot to murder Faribault and McLaughlin. Once he was found guilty, Brave Bear was hanged.

McLaughlin didn't have time to give much thought to Brave Bear's execution. Brave Bear's father-in-law, Sitting Bull, was stirring up a rebellion of his own.

In fact, through a strange twist of fate, McLaughlin's final interaction with Sitting Bull would ruin his reputation. In 1890, McLaughlin was afraid that Sitting Bull was about to flee the area, which could have triggered another series of battles the government didn't want. On December 14, he issued written orders for the chief's arrest. The arresting officers, however, didn't follow those orders to the letter; they decided to force Sitting Bull to ride a horse, rather than putting him in a wagon as McLaughlin had instructed.

The chief refused to comply. His followers were enraged: one shot the arresting officer, who in turn shot Sitting Bull in the chest. A second policeman shot Sitting Bull in the head. More shots were fired, and in the fracas, eight policemen died, along with Sitting Bull and seven of his supporters.

Sitting Bull had been a popular performer in Buffalo's Wild West Show, and his death stirred outrage among white people and Indians alike. In the end, his killing set the stage for a major confrontation at Wounded Knee two weeks later.

While McLaughlin wasn't directly involved in Sitting Bull's death, he was the official who ordered his arrest, and his reputation—after years of work and service among the Indians—was forever tarnished. That was Brave Bear's ultimate revenge, exacted from beyond the grave.

The Grief of The Only One's Wife

Brave Bear's family didn't mourn him, but his friend, The Only One, left a wife who almost went mad with grief.

AT ONE TIME, it was customary for the Native American widows to disfigure themselves when their husbands died, to demonstrate that their sorrow was boundless. In the midst of their grief, they would have no regard for their appearance. In fact, the women would nearly always cut off their hair and scar themselves in some way.

The Only One's wife was one of the most beautiful women on the prairie, but she was a ghastly sight in the days after his death. She tore almost all the clothing from her body. She also tore most of her hair out by the roots. She hacked and gashed at her breasts with a knife, and slashed her legs from the knees to the ankles, and then she walked around the reservation, screaming and covered with blood.

The vision of the bloody widow, wailing and thrashing with grief, haunted James McLaughlin's nightmares for years.

"I don't think that grief could be made to wear a more horrid front than it did that day," he wrote.

Some say the Only One's widow never stopped grieving, even after her hair grew out and her wounds healed. Even now, there are reports of a ghostly Native American woman who roams the old fort, still bleeding, and screaming in mourning for the only man she would ever love.

The Men Who Fell with Custer

Before they died in the Battle of Little Bighorn, several members of the 7th U. S. Cavalry were stationed at Fort Totten. They spent the winter of 1876 barricaded in the fort, stockpiling ammunition, and waiting for news from military headquarters. It was a tense and suspenseful time—and at least one soldier seemed to know that his days were numbered.

Charles Marion Russell, "The Custer Fight" (1903)

ON MARCH 5, a young man named Corporal Thomas P. Eagan wrote to his sister. His command of the English language reflects his youth and lack of formal education.

"We are to start the 10th of this month for the Big horn country," he wrote. "The Indians are getting bad again. I think that we will have some hard times this summer. The old Chief Sitting Bull says that he will not make peace with the whites as long as he had a man to fight. … As soon as I get back of the campaign I will rite you. That is if I do not get my hair lifted by some Indian."

Eagan probably thought he was joking—but he was more prescient than he knew. On June 25, 1876, he was killed in the Battle of Little Bighorn—often referred to as Custer's Last Stand.

All told, two hundred and sixty five men lost their lives that day. Eleven women at Fort Totten were widowed, and the outpost was never the same.

The Soldiers on the Staircase

Be careful when you stand in front of the Captain and First Lieutenant's Quarters at Fort Totten. Don't block the doorway, and if you go inside, don't stand too long at the foot of the stairs—or you might find yourself running into a few men you never expected to meet.

IN ANCIENT GREEK myth, Sisyphus was condemned to push a boulder up a hill, only to watch it roll back down, over and over again.

At Fort Totten, two soldiers have been condemned to their own Sisyphean task, marching up and down a staircase, morning and night, for more than a hundred years.

The stairs are in the Captain's and First Lieutenant's quarters. The building hasn't been restored yet—so while it's open to the public, there's not much to see inside. Open the door, and you'll probably just notice some peeling white walls, a red painted stairwell, and spiders.

Unless, that is, you happen to visit on a day when the soldiers are inside.

Several people have seen two enlisted men in blue Civil War uniforms, making their way down the staircase. They descend a few steps … and then they disappear, fading like smoke on the wind.

The best time to see them is at dawn—when the soldiers who were stationed at the fort would have been heading toward the parade grounds for assembly—or after dark, when they would have been answering the call to quarters.

Some witnesses say the soldiers move soundlessly. Others hear their footsteps on the old wooden stairs. Sometimes, people can even hear a few snippets of conversation, as they discuss "Lincoln," "patrols," and "mail"—three topics that would have consumed much of their living consciousness.

Now that the soldiers are long gone, their consciousness is a matter for speculation. They don't seem to notice tourists and groundskeepers at the site. Every now and then, however, the do seem to linger—almost sadly—just before they glide through the door and fade from view.

The Captain and First Lieutenant's Quarters at Fort Totten

The haunted staircase inside, where observers have seen the ghosts of two Civil War soldiers on the steps

Dear Brother: Michael Vetter's Letters

Time and time again, it's been shown that ghosts truly do want to share their stories with the living. That's especially true in the case of Michael Vetter, a German immigrant who enlisted with the Army and died with Custer at the Battle of Little Bighorn. In the months before his death, he was stationed at Fort Totten, where he wrote a series of letters to his brother in Pittsburgh. In 2004, the Lake Region Pioneer Daughters published some of those letters in a book called The Cowboy Soldier. *The correspondence offers a remarkable glimpse of the mystery that surrounded Devils Lake in the late 1800s—and the letters could reveal while Michael Vetter is still at the fort today, long after he lost his life in Custer's Last Stand.*

MICHAEL VETTER'S LETTERS were always bittersweet.

On New Year's Day, 1876, he wrote to his brother about the holiday celebrations at Fort Totten. He reported that the dining room had been decorated with flags—and he described the revelry that followed Christmas dinner.

"Since there are no girls on the Fort," he wrote, "some of our men dressed as girls and the Dance went on with lots of fun."

He also described the tragic deaths of three of his comrades.

"Dear Brother, some sad case happened some time ago—3 of our men wandered off from the Fort to buy some whiskey. They bought the whiskey all right, —but the guys didn't come home—so a 6 men patrol went out to look for them. They found them too—all three men frozen to death."

It seemed clear that life on the frontier was fraught with danger.

"8 miles from here is a Lake called the 'Devils Lake.' The Indians gave him that name—since so many Indians drowned in there. The Lake has an Island. We can see it from our Fort. One time a sail boat went out to explore the Island—it didn't come back neither … "

Vetter shared good news, too. On January 9, 1876, he wrote, "Dear Brother … we have good warm clothes and plenty good food. My blue overcoat covers even my face."

At one point, his description of the army post read like a school report. "Dear Brother, Canada is 80 miles away from here. We were last week all the soldiers disinfected for sanitary reason. The temperature is sometime -30 degrees -40 degrees zero. The Fort is built in 2 floors, brick walls, hospital, Officer quarters, bakery warehouse, 3 horse barns with 65-70 horses, 4 rooms, 15 men per room. The rooms are 36 feet long and have a big stove for heating. Outside in the middle of yard is the Flagstand—from there is always the Red, White and Blue waving. A full set uniform cost 15 dollar. We go on guard in the night for 2 hours and daytime the sentry duty is 4 hours."

And on January 16, he added a note about the soldiers' off hours.

"Dear Brother, I like to tell you how we sleep … each has a bunk with straw mattress 3-4 blanket to hold you warm, in middle is a big stove, a table with benches. Right now we have very little to do except in the evening we have to take care of the horses. Each soldier besides having a horse has to take care of a gun, a pistol, a sabre, prairie-knife."

A few weeks later, he posted his last letter to his brother from Fort Totten—because he was being transferred to Fort Lincoln, two hundred miles to the west. From there he would join the Seventh Cavalry, for Custer's Last Stand against the Indians.

But Michael Vetter would be back. Even though he died during the Battle of Little Bighorn, he had a mission to finish at Fort Totten.

Today, if you stand very quietly in the old quarters of Fort Totten, you might catch a glimpse of him, still seated at a writing desk in his old company barracks.

Michael Vetter is still trying to finish the letters he never sent.

As nearly as anyone can tell, his death took him by surprise. His rifle didn't fire as it should have, and he was hit by a blinding white light. He was knocked off his horse, and he drowned in a pool of blood.

The pain of his fall dissipated slowly as he walked away from the battlefield and back to his old post at Devils Lake, where he had left a letter to his brother, unfinished.

These days, he's most active after dark, because the light still hurts his eyes. He writes by spectral candle light; visitors see him only as a gleam of silver, like a beam of moonlight.

And while Michael Vetter is grateful for the fact that many of his letters have been preserved, he won't leave the fort until he finishes the last letter home.

The Haunted Little Theatre

Every July, amateur actors perform Broadway productions in a tiny community theater carved from the old schoolroom and barracks of Fort Totten. It's not the kind of place most of them would want to be caught dead in alone, however—and there are usually a few audience members who haven't paid the price of their admission.

The specters are well known to the theater people, who often sense that they're being watched—even when they're not on stage.

IN 1963, TICKETS went on sale for *Oklahoma*, the first production at Fort Totten Little Theatre. Ever since then, local performers have staged summer productions of Broadway musicals. Their talent and enthusiasm have made the venue the longest-running stock theater in the state.

Actors are a superstitious lot under the best of circumstances, but company players at the Fort Totten Little Theatre have good reason to be concerned. Most of them, in fact, choose not to go into the building by themselves—especially if there's no production scheduled.

Ask a few questions, though, and you'll soon learn that no cast or crew member ever really feels alone in the Fort Totten Little Theatre. Instead, someone is always following them, skittering from corner to corner, just out of sight. The players hear strange shuffling sounds, like children running in their stocking feet, as well as muffled laughter in the dressing areas. Once in a while, they hear weeping, like a lost child crying for her mother.

Even when the whole cast is assembled, though, there's no guarantee that the noises will stop. In fact, most know that the odd occurrences will increase. On some nights, costumes are rearranged on the racks. Small containers of stage makeup occasionally disappear, so the actors make do with cosmetics from home. When the performers come back the next day, they find their makeup laid neatly on the counter. And during dress rehearsals, when the lights are shining in their eyes, the actors sense a ghostly audience watching them from the empty auditorium.

The theater itself is in a building that used to be part of the Indian boarding school at the fort. Some children died there, victims of an influenza outbreak that swept the countryside.

68   The Ghosts of Devils Lake

School children play in an early postcard view of the Indian school at Fort Totten

It's possible that some of them are still rebelling against the nuns and teachers who took them from their parents, and unknowingly condemned them to a feverish death.

Others take a brighter view: the ghosts are children, after all, and they're simply being entertained.

Little Fish and the Indians of Fort Totten

The Fort Totten Indian Reservation was established in 1867. Back then, it was called the Cut Head Sioux Indian Reservation. Today, it's known as the Spirit Lake Nation.

The first Indian to settle there was a charismatic chief named Tiowaste "Goodhouse"—also known as Little Fish.

WHILE FORT TOTTEN was primarily a military post to defend overland travel routes, it also played a role in the government's plan to place Indians on reservations and transition them from hunting to farming.

When Fort Totten was established, however, there were no Indians actually living full-time in the area. The Dakota people hunted and camped near Devils Lake every year, but they were migratory; they followed wild game across a huge swath of Dakota Territory.

Thousands of Dakota Indians had also made their way to Devils Lake after the Indian Uprising in Minnesota in 1862, but they had been chased out of the area by Henry Sibley and Alfred Sully.

During the winter of 1868, the Dakota people were camped along the Mouse River, near present-day Minot, North Dakota. Two traders and an interpreter traveled to them and invited the Sioux to come into the fort. At the time, the Dakota people didn't have many options. They were starving, and life at Fort Totten seemed their best hope of survival.

In August 1867, Chief Tiowaste "Goodhouse"—also known as Little Fish—came onto the reservation with more than two hundred warriors. Earlier, he had surrendered his band of fighters from the Dakota Conflict to a garrison at Ryan's Hill, near Fort Totten. At the time, he was afraid they would be mistaken for a band of Sioux under Rain-in-the-Face, who had caused nothing but trouble at the fort, so he sent a special translator ahead to announce their arrival.

By 1870, more than seven hundred Dakota were living there. Like many of them, Little Fish settled into farming. He also worked as a teamster.

"The Indians, generally, on this reservation, have given up many of their old customs and habits and donned the apparel of the whites," a historian wrote at the time. "A few of the older chiefs are loath to give up their Indian finery and the trappings of rank. Wanata, the hereditary chief, still dresses in the ancient garb of his race. The young men and maidens are gradually adopting the dress and the manners of the whites. The older (women) wear beads, tinsel jewelry and moccasins.

"Among the Indians are about three hundred farmers, each occupying with his family a home of his own, generally a log cabin, which the women keep in very neat order," Andreas continued. "Many of them are furnished with carpets, chairs and upholstered furniture, and there is as much outward appearance of prosperity as can be seen around the average pioneer home of the white settler.

"In the place of the Indian marriage ceremonies they have adopted that of the white people, and the priest generally officiates at their weddings. They have adopted the burial system of the whites, and a huge wooden cross marks the cemetery devoted to the burial of their dead."

Little Fish was born in Dakota Territory in the late 1820s. His mother was a Dakota Indian, and his father was a French fur trader.

Little Fish fought his way to the top of his tribe, usually by going into battle against the Ojibwe people. During the Minnesota uprising of 1862, he joined in the attacks on Fort Abercrombie, and for the next five years, he was a fugitive.

Finally, Little Fish decided to turn himself in, and he spent the rest of his life at Fort Totten.

He never really left.

During his first few years on the reservation, Little Fish struggled to adjust to a new culture and a new way of life. Eventually, he learned to farm and build cabins. He watched the railroad reach across the prairie and bring new settlers onto the land. Before he died in 1919, he even learned to drive his own car. Throughout his life, Little Fish was a popular, charismatic figure. According to tribal historian Louis Garcia, Little Fish was a prominent figure at all the celebrations. He led the parade at Chautauqua at Fort Totten from 1893 well into the new century.

Today, you can still see him at the tribe's annual pow wow and special events—especially if you look through the crowd, and pay attention to movement in the corner of your eye. He's the dapper old man in the tailored suit and stovepipe hat, with the King George medal around his neck.

Ignatius Court and the Indian School

There has always been a school at Fort Totten. When it was first built, a group of missionary nuns moved in from Canada to share the gospel with Native American children. And while most people agree that the school was a source of pain and suffering for the parents and children who were separated, the story of a young Dakota boy named Ignatius Court is one of the bright lights in an otherwise heartrending history.

THE GRAY NUNS, a teaching and nursing order from Montreal, came to Fort Totten in the early 1880s. By all accounts, they were selfless people: no ordinary women would brave the western frontier if they didn't believe they were doing some good.

It's also true that the Indians needed help to deal with their forced adjustment to life on a reservation. By government order, Native American children had been taken from their parents, dressed in European-style clothing, and forbidden to speak their native language. The nuns offered the support of their faith during that transition.

But the forced separations lasted far longer than they should have. When the military closed the fort in 1890, the government turned the buildings over to the Department of the Interior, and the school moved in. From that point on, the fort was in almost continuous use as a school until 1959.

Today, tourist photos of the site often capture strange, glowing orbs that aren't visible to the naked eye. Tribal elders who see the photos recognize the lights for what they are: the spirits of Indian mothers, separated from their youngsters, searching for their lost sons and daughters.

That's not the only sign of spirit activity at the school. In the former boys' dormitory at the fort, shadows walk through a closed door into a room that hasn't been used for 50 years.

Other visitors report feelings of overwhelming sadness at the site, especially in the hallways and darkened corners. Some people have actually seen the ghostly round face of a small girl, peering from a second-floor window overlooking Cavalry Square. Others have heard her crying when the wind blows from the south.

Even so, there's at least one success story to report from the site. It comes to us from a boy named Ignatius Court, whose love of learning helped preserve Dakota culture for future generations.

Jerome Hunt could have ministered anywhere he chose. He was a tall and handsome Catholic priest, with a baritone delivery that charmed everyone he met.

But Father Jerome felt a kinship with Native Americans, so he traveled from Saint Louis to Devils Lake in the late 1870s. He set to work learning and preserving the Dakota language. He recorded every word for posterity. He published Indian newspapers and religious tracts, because he believed in the power of the written word to transform an entire Indian nation.

He couldn't have done the work without the help of his favorite pupil, Ignatius Court. In fact, if it hadn't been for Ignatius and his mentor, local Dakota tradition could have been lost forever.

For his part, Ignatius was happy to help. At first, he was simply glad to get out of hauling wood at the fort. The more he stayed inside, however, the more he learned to love the work he shared with his teacher. He grew to love the logic and organization of language in any form.

Ignatius was a natural storyteller, and he shared his stories with Father Jerome. On dark winter nights, Ignatius' older relatives would come in and share their stories, too.

In 1880, Father Jerome brought Ignatius to the office of the *Devils Lake News* to learn the printing trade. For a while, Ignatius and Father Jerome printed a Dakota-language newspaper there. Later, Father Jerome managed to get a hand press for the mission, so he and Ignatius could print a monthly newspaper on the reservation.

Father Jerome and his protégé also published three books in the Dakota language: *The Wowapi Wakan* a bible history, in 1897, *The Catholic Wocekiye Wowapi,* a prayer book with instructions and hymns in 1899, and a second prayer book in 1907.

They completed their work just in time. By the beginning of the twentieth century, the government was focused on assimilation, and the school had three goals: to teach English to Native American children, to train them in farming, and to teach them the basic principles of American history and democracy.

Ignatius Court is one of the few Fort Totten ghosts to leave his voice in writing, so he can speak directly to countless generations still to come.

Rain in the Face

Ghosts tend present an idealized version of themselves. That's especially true in the case of our next visitor, an imposing warrior who wore a fringed leather jacket and an eagle-feather headdress that hung almost to the floor.

ONE OF THE greatest Dakota warriors of all times was Itiomagaju, or "Rain-in-the-Face"—a stocky, muscular fighter with a thirst for adventure and a taste for blood. He was famous for his attacks on soldiers and white settlers, and he helped defeat Custer in the Battle of Little Bighorn.

One of his favorite exploits, however, was his first attempt to disrupt a military outpost—and it just happened to be an attack on Fort Totten, on the southern shores of Devils Lake.

He wasn't afraid of armed soldiers or settlers, any more than he was afraid of the Cheyenne fighters who gave him his name. What's more, until his dying day, he believed that Native Americans who lived on reservations were little more than prisoners.

While he died a broken man, herded into the system he hated, his soul roams free now—and often returns to the site of his first adventure.

Charles A. Eastman, a doctor who worked for the Office of Indian Affairs, spoke to Rain-in-the-Face in 1905, shortly before he died. Eastman's account of their conversation was published in his 1918 book, *Indian Heroes and Great Chieftains*.

These are his words:

About two months before his death I went to see him for the last time, where he lay upon the bed of sickness from which he never rose again, and drew from him his life-history. It had been my experience that you cannot induce an Indian to tell a story, or even his own name, by asking him directly.

"Friend," I said, "even if a man is on a hot trail, he stops for a smoke! In the good old days, before the charge there was a smoke. At home, by the fireside, when the old men were asked to tell their brave deeds, again the pipe was passed. So come, let us smoke now to the memory of the old days!"

Rain-in-the-Face

He took of my tobacco and filled his long pipe, and we smoked. Then I told an old mirthful story to get him in the humor of relating his own history.

The old man lay upon an iron bedstead, covered by a red blanket, in a corner of the little log cabin. He was all alone that day; only an old dog lay silent and watchful at his master's feet. Finally he looked up and said with a pleasant smile:

"True, friend; it is the old custom to retrace one's trail before leaving it forever! I know that I am at the door of the spirit home.

"I was born near the forks of the Cheyenne River, about seventy years ago. My father was not a chief; my grandfather was not a chief, but a good hunter and a feast-maker. On my mother's side I had some noted ancestors, but they left me no chieftainship. I had to work for my reputation.

"When I was a boy, I loved to fight," he continued. "In all our boyish games I had the name of being hard to handle, and I took much pride in the fact.

"I was about ten years old when we encountered a band of Cheyennes. They were on friendly terms with us, but we boys always indulged in sham fights on such occasions, and this time I got in an honest fight with a Cheyenne boy older than I. I got the best of the boy, but he hit me hard in the face several times, and my face was all spattered with blood and streaked where the paint had been washed away. The Sioux boys whooped and yelled:

"'His enemy is down, and his face is spattered as if with rain! Rain-in-the-Face! His name shall be Rain-in-the-Face!'

"Afterwards, when I was a young man, we went on a warpath against the Gros Ventres. We stole some of their horses, but were overtaken and had to abandon the horses and fight for our lives. I had wished my face to represent the sun when partly covered with darkness, so I painted it half black, half red. We fought all day in the rain, and my face was partly washed and streaked with red and black: so again I was christened Rain-in-the-Face. We considered it an honorable name.

"I had been on many war paths, but was not especially successful until about the time the Sioux began to fight with the white man. One of the most daring attacks that we ever made was at Fort Totten, North Dakota, in the summer of 1866.

"Hohay, the Assiniboine captive of Sitting Bull, was the leader in this raid. Wapaypay, the Fearless Bear, who was afterward hanged at Yankton, was the bravest man among us. He dared Hohay to make the charge. Hohay accepted the challenge, and in turn dared the other to ride with him through the agency and right under the walls of the fort, which was well garrisoned and strong.

"Wapaypay and I in those days called each other 'brother-friend.' It was a life-and-death vow. What one does the other must do; and that meant that I must be in the forefront of the charge, and if he is killed, I must fight until I die also!

"I prepared for death. I painted as usual like an eclipse of the sun, half black and half red."

His eyes gleamed and his face lighted up remarkably as he talked, pushing his black hair back from his forehead with a nervous gesture.

"Now the signal for the charge was given! I started even with Wapaypay, but his horse was faster than mine, so he left me a little behind as we neared the fort. This was bad for me, for by that time the soldiers had somewhat recovered from the surprise and were aiming better.

"Their big gun talked very loud, but my Wapaypay was leading on, leaning forward on his fleet pony like a flying squirrel on a smooth log! He held his rawhide shield on the right side, a little to the front, and so did I. Our war whoop was like the coyotes singing in the evening, when they smell blood!

"The soldiers' guns talked fast, but few were hurt. Their big gun was like a toothless old dog, who only makes himself hotter the more noise he makes," he remarked with some humor.

"How much harm we did I do not know, but we made things lively for a time; and the white men acted as people do when a swarm of angry bees get into camp. We made a successful retreat, but some of the reservation Indians followed us yelling, until Hohay told them that he did not wish to fight with the captives of the white man, for there would be no honor in that. There was blood running down my leg, and I found that both my horse and I were slightly wounded.

≈

Two months after he told his life story to Charles Eastman, Rain-in-the-Face died, a broken man, alone in his bed on a South Dakota reservation.

His last words still echo across the prairie.

"I have lived peaceably ever since we came upon the reservation," he said. "No one can say that Rain-in-the-Face has broken the rules of the Great Father. I fought for my people and my country. When we were conquered I remained silent, as a warrior should. Rain-in-the-Face was killed when he put down his weapons before the Great Father. His spirit was gone then; only his poor body lived on, but now it is almost ready to lie down for the last time. Ho, hechetu! It is well."

In old photos, Rain-in-the-Face looks stocky and tight-lipped—but his mouth also turns up, just a bit, as if he was always about to break into a grin. He still looks that way.

If you're lucky enough to visit North Dakota's Fort Totten, watch for him. He appears fleetingly, at first—a stocky warrior in fringed leather and moccasins. He still carries a war staff, with his face painted red and black, like an eclipse of the moon. Say nothing, and you can watch him outside the gates as he relives his moment of glory, again, and again, and again.

Mrs. Faribault's Fresh-Baked Bread

During the 1880s, Fort Totten also boasted its share of strong women.

At first, the only women on the site were officers' wives and daughters, along with servants and laundresses, called "camp followers" by the military. Then the government tried to recruit the most unattractive women they could, in an effort to keep them from marrying the enlisted men. One ad in an eastern newspaper asked for "the most bucktoothed, bow-legged women that can be found!" Eventually, they gave up, and the percentage of males and females at the fort began to resemble a more normal civilian population.

TURN-OF-THE-CENTURY settlements usually smelled like campfire smoke, bacon grease, and coffee. From the time Euphrasine Faribault arrived, however, Fort Totten smelled like fresh-baked bread. Today she uses that scent to signal her presence.

George and Euphrasine Faribault were one of the most prominent couples at the Devils Lake Indian Agency. George was the head farmer, and it was his job to turn Dakota hunters into farmers, too. He distributed their rations, and he taught them how to grow the crops they would need to survive within the reservation's boundaries.

Until the Faribaults arrived, the Indians hadn't been impressed by the flour the government offered them. It wasn't uncommon for them to dump it on the ground and walk away with the flour sacks, just for the cloth to make clothing.

When Euphrasine made her fresh-baked bread, however, no one could turn it down.

For Euphrasine, bread was symbolic. It represented her Christian faith, just as it had signified Christ's teachings for centuries.

She had learned to bake bread from her mother, a quiet evangelist who shared her faith with the Indians.

Euphrasine's maiden name was St. Antoine. She was born in the mid-1880s and raised near Minnesota's Fort Snelling. When she was a young girl, her father moved the family to the Red River Valley in eastern North Dakota, where he was the first man to plant wheat.

George and Euphrasine Faribault's wedding photo. Left to right, top: Alexander Faribault and Father Augustin Ravoux. Left to right, bottom: George Faribault, Euphrasine St. Antoine Faribault, and Jean Baptiste Faribault.

"On one Christmas," Euphrasine remembered, "my mother had cooked and cooked all day, and towards night she took some cotton cloth, and fastened it up to make a kind of altar; using pines and evergreens and candles, and to make the yard bright and cheerful, she put out dishes with lard in them to burn, and when her simple decorations were completed, she got the Indians to come in and then explained it all to them, telling them of the Child Jesus, and his birthday.

"From that time," says Mrs. Faribault, "mother's whole soul was in the work among the Indians; and she was the first woman to tell them of the true God."

After a few years her father moved the family back to Minnesota. Euphrasine married George, the son of a Fort Snelling trader, and settled into government life.

As more and more white families moved to Fort Totten, Euphraisne found herself reaching out to them with her baked goods, too.

Some of the families were destined to suffer unspeakable loss. "I was talking with the priest one day," she told one historian, "and someone came up to me saying, 'There are some soldiers at the door that want to see you.' I turned and went out, and there stood a sergeant and three soldiers.

"Extending his hand to me the Sergeant said, 'Mrs. Faribault, allow me to come in the name of our company, to thank you for all your kindness to us, poor soldiers; remember us in your prayers. 'We'll never forget what you have done, and all you have been to us.'"

A day later, the men left to join Custer's expedition to the Battle of Little Bighorn. None of them survived; Euphrasine was left to help eleven widows through their grief.

These days, fort Totten is a historic site. Few people bake bread there anymore, even in the restored period-style kitchens. For some reason, however, it's not uncommon to smell fresh-baked bread at the site. The scent is fleeting, and it drifts away on the wind within a minute or two.

More than a century since she left, it's Euphrasine Faribault's way of reaching out to welcome visitors to her former home.

The Ghost of Grand Harbor

During the 1880s, Grand Harbor was no place for a woman—especially a pregnant woman.

Like most places in the Devils Lake region, it was open, untamed prairie, where wild grasses grew tall and thick—in some cases, so tall that even a man on horseback could barely see the horizon. In the summer, the undulating ocean of grass baked and turned golden brown under an unrelenting sun. In the winter, the land was buried by mounds and drifts of snow that made travel impossible, even for short distances.

The risk of death was ever present—but the first white woman to die in the Devils Lake region left a lasting legacy.

DEDERICK TONSETH DECIDED to homestead in Grand Harbor in the fall of 1882, determined to tame a few acres of the prairie for himself.

His wife accompanied him all the way to Fargo—but she refused to go further unless he could guarantee a doctor for the delivery of their child. While Dederick quickly dug a one-room shelter into the hollow of a hillside to serve as a temporary home, he also managed to convince Henry Hale, Fort Totten's hospital steward, to attend the birth.

During the last month of his wife's pregnancy, Dederick also arranged for his older sister Dorothy to move in with the young couple, so she could help his wife.

Dorothy worked tirelessly. She cooked, cleaned, carried water, and cared for her Dederick's wife. She did laundry by hand, melting snow in a cast-iron pot before she washed clothes in a wooden tub. She made biscuits from coarsely ground flour and brewed coffee in a tin pot. She worked from sunrise to sunset—never stopping to rest, and never uttering a word of complaint.

At long last, in the middle of a blizzard, Dederick's wife went into labor. Henry Hale wrote about the event in his memoirs.

"Some time in the latter part of March," he wrote, "when the snow was very deep and badly drifted and during a severe blizzard in which no one would care to be out, Mr. Tonseth appeared at my house early in the morning, having walked the distance over the drifts on skis and wanted me to attend his

Some early settlers built sod homes, quickly and easily assembled from strips of prairie turf.

wife. His home was between five and six miles to the north in the direction from which the blizzard was coming. I demurred at first as it was impossible to see very far against the wind, but on his assurance that he could lead my pony and that the snow had been frozen hard so we would not break through, I consented to go. Mr. Tonseth evidently had a good sense of direction as he made a straight line from my house to his."

As they crossed the snow and ice of Devils Lake, he wrote, "all I could see in front of me was Tonseth holding my pony's bridle."

Luckily, the two men arrived at the Tonseth homestead in plenty of time for the baby's birth. Dederick's wife was still in labor, and Dorothy was at her side.

In the hours leading up to the delivery, however, Hale noticed that Dorothy seemed seriously ill. Her high-necked blouse and ankle-length skirts couldn't hide the fact that her bones were practically poking through her skin. Her face was ashen, and there were dark circles under her eyes.

During the delivery, Dorothy boiled washcloths and wrung them out with bony, blue-veined hands. She offered sips of water to Dederick's wife—shaking and trembling herself, in the process. While the little group watched and waited nervously for the baby's birth, Dorothy even prepared biscuits and bacon for breakfast.

At long last, a healthy baby boy was born. Henry Hale stayed long enough to ensure that mother and child were both resting comfortably on a straw tick—a coarse cotton mattress, stuffed with sweet-smelling grasses from the rolling prairie outside.

As he saddled his horse for the ride back to the fort, Henry Hale asked Mr. Tonseth how long his sister had been sick.

"Sick?" he replied. "I didn't know she was sick. She hasn't complained about anything."

At that very moment, however, Dorothy was collapsing into her own bed, sweating, shivering, and drawing short, painful breaths.

She died the next morning.

Dorothy had given every ounce of her strength to ensure that her nephew could come into the world. She had sacrificed her own health for the health of an unborn child.

The baby never knew his aunt—but for years after her death, the young boy often mentioned that an invisible friend named "Dee" followed him around the farm and watched him play.

The Guardian of the Grand Army of the Republic

If you happen to be one of those who are brave enough to walk through the local cemetery at night, you're sure to encounter some of the ghosts of Devils Lake.

They're just as accessible during the day—especially if you make your way into the oldest part of the cemetery, where loyal veterans of the Grand Army of the Republic are buried.

DURING THE WESTWARD expansion of the United States, hundreds of soldiers found themselves blazing a path into Dakota Territory. Some decided to stay—forever. Today they lie together near the life-size statue of a young infantryman, dressed in uniform, carrying his trusty Springfield musket, and guarding their graves for eternity. They had the granite monument carved before they died, inscribed with the words that guided them in life: loyalty, charity, and fraternity.

Some say the statue is more than a block of granite. Some say it serves as a physical receptacle for the souls of those old soldiers. His watchful eyes are their eyes, and they all take turns defending the field of the fallen.

On moonlit nights, some swear that the statue even seems to move. Those who have seen it report that the statue moves slightly from side to side, as if the young soldier is shifting the weight on his feet. His shoulders shrug, almost imperceptibly, and he changes his grip on his rifle. But the strangest reports of all claim that even when the statue stands perfectly still, the eyes move, constantly scanning the horizon for any threats to the peace of the grave.

The statue most closely resembles a young Alonzo Bartlett, who was born in New York in 1843. Both of his parents died when he was still young, and he and his younger brother and sister were orphaned.

Alonzo enlisted in the New York 35th infantry, Company I. He mustered in on June 11, 1861, and mustered out almost two years later, on June 5, 1863.

Civil War soldiers were some of the first white settlers in Devils Lake.

The 1,250-man regiment left New York in early July, 1861, and served in Virginia and Washington, D. C. For a time the men did construction work on Forts Tillinghast and Craig. They passed the winter of 1861 camped in Fall's Church. The regiment participated in the second battle of Bull Run, South Mountain, and Antietam. Forty four men were killed in battle, and fifty six died as a result of accidents, imprisonment, or disease.

After the war, Alonzo and his brother Charles homesteaded in Iowa. He was married three times there, and he had five sons. He spent his final years in Devils Lake, living with his son Howard and daughter-in-law Ethal on his Civil War pension. According to his war records, he had a lifetime of health issues due to injuries he received during the Civil War. He died at home, but then was transferred to his permanent post with the rest of the Grand Army of the Republic.

The Cowboy's Lament

If you're looking for a soundtrack for life in Devils Lake, you can't do much better than this traditional folk song—which many area residents have taken to heart. The lyrics date back to the 1800s.

"O bury me not on the lone prairie."
These words came low and mournfully
From the pallid lips of the youth who lay
On his dying bed at the close of day.

He had wasted and pined 'til o'er his brow
Death's shades were slowly gathering now.
He thought of home and loved ones nigh,
As the cowboys gathered to see him die.

"O bury me not on the lone prairie,
Where coyotes howl and the wind blows free
In a narrow grave just six by three—
O bury me not on the lone prairie.

"It matters not, I've been told,
Where the body lies when the heart grows cold.
Yet grant, o grant, this wish to me—
O bury me not on the lone prairie.

"I've always wished to be laid when I died,
In a little churchyard on the green hillside.
By my father's grave, there let me be,
O bury me not on the lone prairie.

"I wish to lie where a mother's prayer
And a sister's tear will mingle there.
Where friends can come and weep o'er me.
O bury me not on the lone prairie.

"For there's another whose tears will shed
For the one who lies in a prairie bed.
It breaks me heart to think of her now,
She has curled these locks, she has kissed this brow."

"O bury me not …" And his voice failed there.
But they took no heed to his dying prayer.
In a narrow grave, just six by three,
They buried him there on the lone prairie.

And the cowboys now as they roam the plain,
For they marked the spot where his bones were lain,
Fling a handful o' roses o'er his grave
With a prayer to God his soul to save.

The Devil's Heart

ONE OF THE most mysterious places in the Devils Lake region is Devil's Heart, a tall hill on the Spirit Lake Indian reservation. You can see it for miles, rising almost two hundred feet above fields and pastures. The Dakota people called it Chantee Hill, because *chantee* meant "heart" or "center" of the region.

For generations of Dakota Indians, Devil's Heart was a traditional meeting place to discuss war, hunting, or other ventures. They said that any promise made on the hill was sacred—and that violations and deceptions would be punished by suffering and death.

Father J. B. Genin, one of the first missionaries in the area, tried to claim the hill for Christianity. He erected a cross at the summit in 1868. At the time, he declared that the lake was to be known as Saint Michael's Lake—but the change was never adopted.

That might be because Father Genin wasn't the only holy man on Devil's Heart that day. Directly under his feet lay the bones of Chotanka, a long-lost spiritual leader whose stories live on to this day.

One of those stories begins on the next page.

Chotanka, the Bear Man

Chotanka was a compelling storyteller. For years, he told his followers that he wasn't always a man. In fact, he said, he had been born a grizzly bear, and he lived the life of a wild animal until a beautiful woman lured him into her tent and transformed him into a man. Chotanka's story of life as a bear is bizarre—but mesmerizing, because he describes mankind from a bear's point of view.

This story, about a race around Devils Lake, was so popular that his followers kept it alive long after Chotanka himself was dead and buried on the hill he helped make famous. On a clear night, you might even be able to hear it from Chotanka himself—if you climb to the top of Devil's Heart and listen carefully.

BACK WHEN I was a bear, my home was in sight of the Mini-wakan Chantay—the hill you know as Devil's Heart. I lived with my mother only one winter, and I only saw my father when I was a baby.

In my earliest memory of life as a bear cub, I was playing outside of our home with a buffalo skull that I had found nearby. I saw something that looked strange. It was a man. He walked upon two legs, and he carried a crooked stick, and some red willows with feathers tied to them. I learned later that they were arrows. He threw one of the willows at me, and I showed my teeth and retreated to our den.

Just then my father and mother came home with a buffalo calf. They were both imposing, huge bears. They threw down the dead calf and ran after the man. He had long hair upon a round head. His face was round, too. He ran and climbed up into a small oak tree.

My father and mother shook him down, but not before he had shot some of his red willows into their sides. Mother was very sick, but she dug some roots and ate them and she was well again. That's how I was first taught the use of certain roots for curing wounds and sickness.

One day, when I was out hunting with my mother—my father had gone away and never came back—we found a buffalo cow with her calf in a ravine. My mother advised me to follow her closely, and we crawled along on our knees.

All at once mother crouched down under the grass, and I did the same. We saw some of those queer men again. At that time, we called them 'two legs.' They were riding on ponies that looked like big-tail deer.

A vintage engraved illustration of an American black bear from the Trousset Encyclopedia *(1886 - 1891)*

They yelled as they rode toward us. Mother growled terribly and rushed upon them. She caught one, but many more came with their dogs and drove us into a thicket. They sent their arrows of red willows singing after us, and two of them stuck in mother's side.

When we got away at last she tried to pull them out, but they hurt her terribly. She pulled them both out at last, but soon after she lay down and died.

Now an orphaned bear cub, Chotanka learned to fend for himself.

I stayed in the woods alone for two days; then I went around the Mini-wakan Chantay on the south side and there made my lonely den. There I found plenty of hazel nuts, acorns and wild plums. Upon the plains food was abundant, and I saw nothing of my enemies.

One day I found a paw print not unlike my own. I followed it to see who the stranger might be. Upon the bluffs among the oak groves, I discovered beautiful young female, gathering acorns. She was of a different band from mine, for she wore a jet black dress.

Her name was Woshepee. At first she resented my intrusion, but when I told her of my lonely life she agreed to share it with me. We came back to my home on the south side of the hill. There we lived happy for a whole year. When the autumn came again, Woshepee said that she must make a warm nest for the winter, and I was left alone again.

One day, a mythic figure challenged the young bear to a race.

All the long winter I slept in my den, and with the early spring there came a great thunder storm. I was aroused by a frightful crash that seemed to shake the hills.

Suddenly, a handsome young man stood at my door. I looked, but I wasn't afraid, for I saw that the stranger carried none of those red willows with feathered tips. He was unarmed and smiling.

"I come," said he, "with a challenge to run a race. Whoever wins will be the hero of his kind, and the defeated must do as the winner says thereafter. This is a rare honor that I have brought you. The whole world will see the race. The animal world will shout for you, and the spirits will cheer me on. You are not a coward, and therefore you will not refuse my challenge."

I studied the man before I answered. He looked strong, but he was lightly built. I agreed to race against him.

"We shall start from the Chantay," he said, "and we will run around the lake, back to our start. Come; let us go, for the universe is waiting!"

Before the race began, another stranger appeared—this time, with a warning.

As the stranger started off to the hill, an old wrinkled man came to my door. He leaned forward upon his staff.

"My son,' he told me, 'I don't want to make you a coward, but this young man is the greatest gambler of the universe. He is a spirit from heaven, and those whom he outruns must shortly die. He gambles for life itself—but he is always safe, for if he is killed, he can resurrect himself. I tell you, he has powerful medicine."

The old man looked at me intently, and then continued speaking.

"My brothers and I are the only ones who have ever beaten him,' he said. 'I think that I can save you, too. Listen carefully. He will run behind you all the way until you are within a short distance of the goal. Then he will pass you by in a flash, for his name is Zig-Zag Fire. Yes, he is lightning itself.

"Here is my medicine," the old man continued. He handed me a rabbit skin and the gum of a certain plant. 'When you come near the goal, rub yourself with the gum, and throw the rabbit skin between you. That way, he cannot pass you."

I asked him, "Who are you, grandfather?"

"I am the medicine turtle," the old man replied. You have heard, no doubt, that all animals know beforehand when they are to be killed, and any man who understands these mysteries may also know when he is to die."

I had no intention of dying, so I gladly accepted the old man's help.

Thousands gathered to watch the race. Animals came to cheer for Chotanka; mystic spirits came to encourage Zig-Zag fire.

The race was announced to the world. The buffalo, elk, wolves, and all the animals came to look on. All the spirits of the air came also to cheer for their comrade.

In the sky the trumpet was sounded, and the great medicine drum was struck on earth. It was the signal for our start.

We started running the course around the lake. Everywhere the multitude cheered as we sped by.

Just as the old man had told me, Zig-Zag Fire stayed behind me until we had almost reached the Chantay, and the finish line was in sight. At that point, I felt a slight shock. That's when I knew it was time to throw my rabbit skin back.

And just as the old man had said, Zig-Zag Fire tripped and fell. I rubbed myself with the gum, and I ran on until I reached the goal.

There was a great shout that echoed over the earth, but in the heavens there was muttering and grumbling. The referee declared that I would live to a good old age, and Zig-Zag Fire promised to come at my call. He was indeed great medicine.

The Animal People of Devil's Heart

While Chotanka was buried on Devil's Heart, the site had an even deeper spiritual significance. According to Dakota legend, it was the site where God turned some tribes of people into animals.

This story comes to us from Charles Alexander Eastman, one of the most unusual figures of the nineteenth and twentieth centuries. Judging by his name, you might think he was a white settler—but he was, in fact, a traditional Dakota Indian. His parents called him Ohiyesa. He was born in Minnesota, raised in Manitoba, Canada, and homesteaded with his father in Dakota Territory. As a young man, he earned a medical degree from Boston University. In 1902, he published Indian Boyhood, *the first of eleven books about life in Indian Territory.*

This is his story.

OLD WEYUHA WAS regarded as the greatest story-teller among the Wahpeton Sioux.

"Tell me, good Weyuha, a legend of your father's country," I said to him one evening, for I knew the country which is now known as North Dakota and Southern Manitoba was their ancient hunting-ground. I was prompted by Uncheedah to make this request, after the old man had eaten in our lodge.

"Many years ago," he began, as he passed the pipe to uncle, "we traveled from the Otter-tail to Minnewakan (Devil's Lake). At that time the mound was very distinct where Chotanka lies buried. The people of his immediate band had taken care to preserve it.

"This mound under which lies the great medicine man is upon the summit of Minnewakan Chantay, the highest hill in all that region. It is shaped like an animal's heart placed on its base, with the apex upward.

"The reason why this hill is called Minnewakan Chantay, or the Heart of the Mysterious Land, I will now tell you. It has been handed down from generation to generation, far beyond the memory of our great-grandparents. It was in Chotanka's line of descent that these legends were originally kept, but when he died the stories became everybody's, and then no one believed in them. It was told in this way."

Charles Alexander Eastman

I sat facing him, wholly wrapped in the words of the story-teller, and now I took a deep breath and settled myself so that I might not disturb him by the slightest movement while he was reciting his tale. We were taught this courtesy to our elders, but I was impulsive and sometimes forgot.

"A long time ago," resumed Weyuha, "the red people were many in number, and they inhabited all the land from the coldest place to the region of perpetual summer time. It seemed that they were all of one tongue, and all were friends.

"All the animals were considered people in those days. The buffalo, the elk, the antelope, were tribes of considerable importance. The bears were a smaller band, but they obeyed the mandates of the Great Mystery and were his favorites, and for this reason they have always known more about the secrets of medicine. So they were held in much honor. The wolves, too, were highly regarded at one time. But the buffalo, elk, moose, deer and antelope were the ruling people.

"These soon became conceited and considered themselves very important, and thought no one could withstand them. The buffalo made war upon the smaller tribes, and destroyed many. So one day the Great Mystery thought it best to change the people in form and in language.

"He made a great tent and kept it dark for ten days. Into this tent he invited the different bands, and when they came out they were greatly changed, and some could not talk at all after that. However, there is a sign language given to all the animals that no man knows except some medicine men, and they are under a heavy penalty if they should tell it.

"The buffalo came out of the darkened tent the clumsiest of all the animals. The elk and moose were burdened with their heavy and many-branched horns, while the antelope and deer were made the most defenseless of animals, only that they are fleet of foot. The bear and the wolf were made to prey upon all the others.

"Man was alone then. When the change came, the Great Mystery allowed him to keep his own shape and language. He was king over all the animals, but they did not obey him. From that day, man's spirit may live with the beasts before he is born a man. He will then know the animal language but he cannot tell it in human speech. He always retains his sympathy with them, and can converse with them in dreams.

"I must not forget to tell you that the Great Mystery pitched his tent in this very region. Some legends say that the Minnewakan Chantay was the tent itself, which afterward became earth and stones. Many of the animals were washed and changed in this lake, the Minnewakan, or Mysterious Water. It is the only inland water we know that is salt. No animal has ever swum in this lake and lived."

"Tell me," I eagerly asked, "is it dangerous to man also?"

"Yes," he replied, "we think so; and no Indian has ever ventured in that lake to my knowledge. That is why the lake is called Mysterious," he repeated.

The Devil's Tooth

A local landmark called the Devil's Tooth is probably one of the largest boulders you'll ever see. It stands about six feet high, and it's five feet square at the base. If you squint and tilt your head a little, you might even see where it gets its name: it looks like a giant tooth with its roots pointing upward.

Today, dry prairie grass grows up around the Devil's Tooth, just as it has for as long as anyone can remember. As you walk toward it, grasshoppers will scramble out of your way, and they'll scratch and poke your legs when they brush past you. You'll hear toads and crickets chirping, and some of them might rustle past you, too. That's all to be expected. But when you get close enough to touch the Devil's Tooth, you'll probably notice that everything changes.

The wind will stop blowing.

The insects will stop making noise.

And if you stand still, a single black crow will come to you.

YEARS AGO, A young Dakota woman named Raven lived near Devils Lake with her husband and child. Like the other women of the tribe, she did what was expected of her: she helped butcher the meat that the men brought back from the hunt. She pounded it into pemmican, picked berries, and moved her family's tent when it was time to go from one hunting spot to another.

She had been born with magic powers, though—powers that often expressed themselves when she least expected it.

She could find springs of cool water just by walking over open land. "I can feel it tingling under my feet," she explained.

She could start fires simply by staring at a dry piece of wood—but that was a trick she saved for emergencies, since it usually frightened anyone who watched.

At night, when she lay in her bed, she could throw sparks from her fingertips. When she waved her hand through the air, she could draw pictures of light in the dark. She used to entertain herself and her daughter that way, for hours, while she waited for her husband to join them in her tipi.

An Indian mother and child, photographed by Edward S. Curtis, 1908

Raven's husband liked to stay out late. He and his friends would sit by the fire and play dice games with stones, shells, or sticks. While others played for fun, her husband's group of friends would place wagers on their games. As time went on, they played longer and longer games, often lasting far into the night.

Sometimes, he wouldn't come home at all.

One morning, Raven woke up to find her husband and one of his friends both leering at her.

"Wake up," he said, "and meet your new husband."

His friend grinned—sneered, actually—curling his top lip in a way she didn't like. She could see all of his teeth, long and yellow, like an animal bearing his fangs.

"You belong to me now," he said. "I won you fair and square."

Raven's husband nodded and put his arm around his friend. They were both wild-eyed and uncoordinated.

"You'll need to make room for my things," the friend added, laughing and pointing at the hunting and fishing tools that were hanging from the tent poles. "I'm moving in."

Raven was incensed. She scooped her child out of bed and stormed out of the tent.

Behind her, the two men started laughing again, this time even louder.

Raven started walking, as fast as she could, away from the camp, and away from her husband's mocking laughter. When she heard the men following her, she started running.

They kept following her, laughing and stumbling and calling her name.

"Raven," her husband shouted. "Come back! Come back! We were just joking. Come on! We were just playing with you."

Raven didn't want to see either of them, but there was no place for her to hide.

As she ran, she searched frantically for a tree, a rock, anything that could shield her from view. There was nothing but grass—tall prairie grass, as high as a horse—but that could only disguise their location for a minute.

Raven had no escape. She fell to the ground, wishing that the earth would simply swallow her up.

Raven's husband and his friend were close behind her. They had seen the top of her head as she crossed over a low rise, but then it disappeared on the other side. Raven's husband still thought he could catch up, apologize, and sweet-talk Raven into returning to the campground with them.

It took them less than a minute to reach the slope—but when they got there, Raven was nowhere to be seen. There was nothing in her place but a giant boulder. From one angle it looks like a tooth—but from another, it's shaped like a woman with a child on her back.

Some say the boulder is Raven herself, locked away in time and space, in a form that can't be damaged or moved. Others say the boulder marks the spot where the earth did, in fact, swallow her up—and that she lives on, safe from her husband, comfortably hidden in a world of darkness and shadow.

The Little People of Devils Lake

The Irish have leprechauns. Germans have elves. Norwegians have trolls, and Greeks and Romans have nymphs. In the hills and fields around Devils Lake, the locals have their own little people to contend with—the Canyo Tina, who make their homes in the trees around the shore.

SINCE THE EARLY 1990s, the waters of Devils Lake have been rising, slowly but surely unleashing a slow-moving flood across the tableau of the prairie.

In 1994, a heavy spring snowfall pushed the lake five feet above its shoreline in just six months—a noticeable change when water spreads out, not up.

Now the lake has doubled in size. The water has claimed thousands of acres of fields and grazing land—along with hundreds of farms, homes, and roadways.

The change has made the activities of the Canyo Tina more visible, too, as they look for new homes on higher ground.

Like other fabled little people, the Canyo Tina are a race of immortals that live in a crossover dimension between the physical and spiritual world. They're about knee-high, with long hair that almost touches the ground. Some are black, some are white, and some are a golden shade of tan. As a general rule, they're gentle creatures—but they don't like to be disturbed.

"The word *Canyo* means woods," Alvina Alberts, a Dakota elder, once told me. "The word *Tina* means '*lives in*.' So the *Canyo Tina* are those who live in the woods."

Years ago, Dakota children would look for the Canyo Tina, but the little people don't always want to be found. That's because they're busy: the Canyo Tina love music and spend most of their time drumming, singing, and dancing.

Sometimes people hear their drums in the hills around Devils Lake—but the elders warn children not to follow the sound. The Canyo Tina don't like to be disturbed, and they'll cast a spell of confusion over people who come too close.

An engraving by W. M. Lizars, based on a painting by Richard Dadd (1873)

Sometimes, the Canyo Tina surprise people by displaying a kind and generous side to their nature. There have been reports from people who have heard small, strange voices outside their homes at night. The next morning they found their fields harvested, as if a whole force of men had been at work.

The Canyo Tina can be helpful—but more often, they're mischievous. They tie clothes to a clothesline when people hang their laundry out to dry. They braid horses' manes and tails into long, fine strands that are almost impossible to comb out. They make thumping noises on the sides of boats, or throw stones into the water when people are trying to fish. Sometimes they even dive under the surface of the lake, and tangle everyone's fishing lines or stick branches to their hooks.

Alvina Alberts, the late tribal elder, offered her advice to those who wander into the Canyo Tinas' realm.

"When a hunter finds anything of value in the woods, like a knife, he's supposed say, 'Little People, I would like to take this,' because it might belong to them—and if he doesn't ask permission, the Canyo Tina will throw stones at him as he goes home. They won't be appeased until someone leaves them an offering of tobacco in the trees."

Their tricks aren't always mean-spirited, though. They look like shadows, and sometimes, they'll sneak into children's bedrooms at night, just to make them laugh in their sleep.

Some Native Americans tell the story of a little boy who, like Peter Pan, never wanted to grow up—until finally, the Canyo Tina took pity on him.

As a young child, he walked around saying that so much that people called him "Forever Boy." When other children talked about everything they would do with their lives, Forever Boy would go off and play by himself.

Eventually his parents got tired of Forever Boy's immaturity. His father got angry, and said, "I'll never call you 'Forever Boy' again. From now on you're going to learn to be a man, you're going to take responsibility for yourself, and you're going to stop playing all day long. You have to learn these things. Starting tomorrow you're going to go to your uncle's, and he's going to teach you everything you'll ever need to know.'"

Forever Boy's heart was broken. He couldn't stand the thought of growing up. He went out to the river and he cried. He cried so hard that he didn't see his animal friends gather around him.

They were trying to tell him something, and they were trying to make him feel better, and finally he thought he understood them say, "Come here tomorrow. Come here early."

He thought they just wanted to say goodbye to him. He was so upset he couldn't sleep.

The next morning he went out early, as he had promised, to meet his friends. When he got to the river, he saw that he was surrounded by the Canyo Tina, who were smiling and laughing and running to hug him.

"Forever Boy," they said. "You don't have to grow up. You can stay with us forever. You can come and be one of us. We'll ask the Creator to send a vision to your parents, so they know that you're safe and doing what you need to do."

Forever Boy thought about it for a long time, and then he went with the Canyo Tina—the little people who are always young at heart.

The Dead Man's Trail

When North Dakota was still the Wild West, carrying the mail was one of the most dangerous jobs in the region. In the early days of Fort Totten, several men who were charged with the job found themselves lying dead in the grass, forced to carry on their mission in spirit form.

DURING THE TUMULTUOUS decade of the 1860s, mail carriers were some of the bravest men on the western frontier. They weren't simply delivering messages and news from points east, like New York and Chicago; they were blazing a trail for civilization and forging a path for generations of settlers.

Unfortunately, they had to risk their lives in the process. They fought their way past wild bears and buffalo stampedes. They stormed through deadly winter blizzards. And perhaps most terrifying of all, they faced the constant threat of Indian attacks.

One of the most dangerous routes in the wild west was the road between Fort Totten, on the southern shore of Devils Lake, and Fort Stevenson, about a hundred miles to the west. In fact, Pierre Bottineau's daughter Marie was married to one of the mail carriers—a Scotchman named McDonald—when warring Indians scalped him.

Another of the mail carriers who traveled that road routinely was a young man named Josh Murphy. In his honor, an anonymous poet christened the route the "Dead Man's Trail."

It was in the spring of sixty-four,
Just a little while ere the war was o'er,
That 'twas mine the mail bags to transport
From Stevenson Pass to Totten fort;
Through the rugged passes the route to take
O'er the mountains that frown on Devils Lake;
Those canyons alive with skulking crews
Of the Chippewas and the savage Sioux;
But my heart felt light and my arm felt strong
For brave Josh Murphy rode along.

Mail carriers like these had the most dangerous job on the frontier.

Josh was shot, and he begged his companion to prevent their attackers from taking his scalp. Charlie lifted the dying man into his saddle, and Josh's pony ran into the night.

> *We sought for Josh and we struck his trail*
> *In the dew damp notes of the scattered mail;*
> *And we found him at last, scarce a pistol shot*
> *From the picket wall of the fort he sought.*
> *There he proudly lay with his unscalped head*
> *On the throbless breast of his pony—dead!*
> *And the route from the pass to the cedared hill*
> *Is known as the 'Deadman's Journey' still.*

Sometimes, when the snow is falling and the wind is still, you can catch a glimpse of Josh Murphy. He forever carries a sack on his back, and trudges through a blanket of snow on the northern prairie. Oddly enough, he leaves no footprints on the Dead Man's Trail.

The Hired Man

A violent mass murder took place not far from Devils Lake, in the tiny hamlet of Cando, North Dakota. That's where a young field hand faced his first romantic rejection, in July of 1893. Rather than leaving quietly, he flew into a rage and viciously slaughtered four young children and their parents—but he left the object of his affection, along with three more youngsters, to bear witness to his crime.

ALFRED BOMBERGER WAS twenty two, and he wanted to marry the farmer's daughter, seventeen-year-old Annie Krieger. She had no interest in him, and her father Daniel was about to send him packing. Instead, Bomberger killed him and his pregnant wife Barbara, as well as three girls and a boy: Bernice, thirteen; Murbey, eleven; Mary, nine; and David, seven. He spared three younger children, Aaron, twelve; Eva, five; and Henry, three.

Bomberger attacked Annie, and when his lust for blood and violence was sated, he forced her to fix him lunch and hand over fifty dollars. Then he fled. Poor Annie was left alone to walk into Cando and report the crime.

Bomberger didn't get far. He was captured in Manitoba, Canada, brought back to justice in North Dakota, and hanged in a field overlooking the scene of his crime.

The surviving children weren't there to witness his death. On the same day as the murders, a neighbor had taken them by train to live with their grandparents in Pennsylvania. The family farm was sold at auction, but for years, the house were the murders took place stood vacant. It eventually burned to the ground in 1917.

This ghostly conversation is based on Annie's handwritten account of the murders, which she filed on the day of the crime.

~

Bernice: My family's house burned to the ground today. After thirty years, I'm free.

Albert: You were always free to go, Bernice … but I'll be tied to that land forever, linked by a rope and a wooden beam.

Alfred Bomberger, mass murderer

Bernice: For five years, I lived there with my father Daniel, my mother Barbara, and my six brothers and sisters. We were Mennonites.

Albert: Mennonites. "Plain people." And yet, you held yourselves above me.

Bernice: I was only thirteen. My sister Murbey was eleven. Mary was nine. And David had just turned seven.

Albert: I was a self-made man. I deserved better.

Bernice: He and father never had any trouble that I knew.

Albert: All I wanted was a little respect.

Bernice: I know he liked us—especially my sister Annie and myself.

Albert: Annie was seventeen. She was old enough to marry.

Bernice: After supper that last night, we all played croquet until it was so dark we could not see. He seemed all right then.

Albert: The old man gave me nothing. Not even the dignity of fair consideration.

Bernice: He started to work for my father last November, I think. Papa asked me if ever Albert was not in my room. I told him that he came in once, but this was some time ago.

Hundreds of people came to see Bomberger hanged for killing six members of a farm family in Cando.

Albert: I knew my place. Others said I was lazy, shiftless, and a complainer, but who were they to judge? They didn't know me.

Bernice: That morning, we were all in bed upstairs. I could hear Mama in the kitchen, peeling potatoes.

Albert: I could not let that man shame me for making a fair request.

Bernice: Albert got up and went downstairs. He got the shotgun, and shot papa first, in papa's bedroom. I heard my mother holler, and he fired again.

Albert: The old man died instantly, but his wife refused to go quietly. I had to cut her throat.

Bernice: He had the gun in his hand and when he got upstairs, he shot three times into the bedroom. He shot Murbey first, and then Mary and David.

Albert: I shot them all in the head. It was painless. Then I hunted for you upstairs, Bernice.

Bernice: I jumped out the window and ran to the barn.

Albert: I found you bridling your pony. I could not let you leave.

Bernice: He took me upstairs and made me watch as he pulled the trigger.

Albert: I realized then that little Mary wasn't dead, so after I took care of Bernice, I went downstairs and got the butcher knife.

Bernice: Annie begged him to leave the youngest children alone.

Albert: I let the babies live. There was no need to upset Annie any more. None of this was her fault.

Bernice: He took Eva, Aaron, and Henry and put them in the southwest room.

Albert: I wish I could have locked the door.

Bernice: He made Annie go into his room, and he told her that he was mad and crazy. He began to take off his clothes, and told her that she knew what he wanted. He made her lie down on the bed. He said he would kill her if she did not lie down there. He then got into bed with her. He forced her.

Albert: It was my right. The old man had no say.

Bernice: He ordered Annie to bring him a basin of water, and then he changed his clothes.

Albert: After I changed, I asked Annie if there was any blood on my clothes. I was clean.

Bernice: He made Annie cook him lunch. While he waited for his food, he rested his feet on our mother's head.

Albert: I was hungry.

Bernice: Our mother was pregnant.

Albert: My work had taken me just a half an hour. I had started at half past six, and got through at seven o'clock.

Bernice: He ate, and then he made Annie get the money in papa's pocket, and papa's gold watch. I don't know how much money she took out of papa's pocket, but there was $50 in a chest, and $1.15 in Annie's bedroom. He took it all.

Albert: I needed cash.

Bernice: He also made Annie get him matches, and the new bridle for the pony. Every time he ordered Annie to do anything he followed her with the gun. She did everything he asked her to do, because he told her he would kill her if she didn't follow his commands.

Albert: I told Annie to get the rifle and shells. She took the spring out and I put the shells in. Then she put the spring back into the rifle, and I shut it up. We worked well together. She would have been a good wife for me.

Bernice: After he got the rifle loaded, he went to the barn and saddled the pony. He took two boxes of cartridges to the barn with him, and the rifle was loaded out of another box.

Albert: I knew I couldn't stay much longer. I took my buffalo coat and put it on the saddle. Annie asked me where I was going, but I didn't know—and I wouldn't tell her even if I did.

Bernice: He told Annie to stay in the barn. Then he went out and looked around.

Albert: Before I left, I tied the girl upstairs.

Bernice: He tied Annie's hands behind her back, and then he tied the rope around her waist. He tied her feet and then he said, "I guess that will hold you a half day. The butcher will be out sometime today and let you loose."

Albert: Before I left, I asked her if she was comfortable. She said that she was fine.

Bernice: Annie freed herself that morning, and walked to town to get help with the three youngest children. That night, our neighbor took them all to the train. He rode back to Pennsylvania with them, so they could live with our grandparents.

Albert: I made my escape to Manitoba.

Bernice: The rest of us were on that train to Pennsylvania, too. Mother, Father, Murbey, Mary, and David. Our bodies were buried five days later, in Lancaster.

Albert: A lynch mob wanted to tie me up in the house and burn it down around me, but the sheriff kept me alive until the hanging.

Bernice: I waited for that fire for thirty years.

Albert: Because of Annie's testimony, I had no choice but to plead guilty.

Bernice: I watched Albert hang for his crimes, in a field facing our farm. At the end, his feet dangled just six inches from the ground.

Albert: I can still see the house. It still stands. Even when I close my eyes, I see it, filled with the bodies of the Kreiger family.

Bernice: But now, at last, it's just an empty field.

The Murder of the Ward Brothers

For a time, Devils Lake represented the best—and the worst—of the Wild West. After the city organized in 1883, a series of "Devils Lake troubles" marked disputes over the city's boundaries and land divisions.

In 1883, an editor at the **Larimore Pioneer** *described the area as a no-man's land of lawlessness. "By their wrangling," he wrote, "they are doing all possible to convince the world at large that theirs is actually the Devil's own country.*

"If they persist in their infernal mobs, shooting scrapes, shanty burnings, etc., people cannot but be convinced that the Devils Lake country is in habited by a band of roughs and that a decent man's life is not safe there. They are fast winning a reputation to vie with Deadwood, Leadville or Virginia City … All respectable people regret to see the settlers of Devils Lake, one of the best portions of the Territory, the one foul blot on Dakota's map."

The lawlessness of Devils Lake reached its peak with the murder of the Ward brothers.

THE DAY BEFORE they were murdered, Fred and Charles Ward rode their horses into Bartlett for cigars.

The village shopkeeper had heard they were in trouble. At that time, the land north of Devils Lake was open to anyone who would farm it, plant trees, and live on their claim. Hundreds of settlers put up shanties to prove that they lived on the land.

"Powerful men want that parcel for themselves," he warned them. "If I were you, I wouldn't go back there tonight."

"Don't worry about us," they replied, laughing—and then they used a popular expression of the time to make light of the situation. "And if we don't see you again 'Then hello.'"

Fred was thirty; he was already established in life, with a wife and child back in Chicago. Charles was twenty seven. Their father was a Chicago doctor, and their uncle owned a department store in the windy city.

Fred also happened to be a graduate of West Point. One of his classmates, Heber Creel, was a second lieutenant in the Seventh Cavalry, and he had encouraged Fred to follow him to Dakota Territory.

The Ward brothers had staked their claim in a shanty like this one.

In 1880, Creel had been stationed at Fort Totten, where he made maps of the lake and the reservation. As the telegraph and the railroad moved closer, he resigned his post and became a speculator, with maps of a town site named Creel City. In the process, he brought in a number of men to help him claim as much of the north shore as possible.

Creel and his associates filed claims—but they also squatted and used legal mumbo-jumbo to convince newcomers that the land was already taken. If those measures didn't work, they resorted to threats and intimidation. By the spring of 1883, they had gained control of several thousand acres.

The Ward brothers had filed claims on four one-hundred-and-sixty-acre tracts near Larimore, and then cast their sights toward Devils Lake. About half way between Creel City and the town of Devils Lake, three miles away, they discovered that one of Creel's men, John Bell, had used his claim shack to straddle two adjoining claims.

The Ward brothers went to the U. S. Land Office in Grand Forks to investigate John Bell's land claim and learned that Bell had legal claim to only one piece of the land. The other parcel was open to contest. Anyone who wanted it simply had to homestead the property for a year.

In April, Fred and Charles built a shanty to claim the open parcel. He and Charles cobbled together a lopsided one-room shack on the desolate section of prairie. They nailed rough wooden boards together, upright, like planks in a fence. The door was crooked and short, and there were no windows in the structure. Its most notable feature was just a tall metal smokestack.

Before long, John Bell heard that he might lose the land to the Ward brothers—but he wouldn't let it go without a fight.

On April 22, John Bell stopped by to demand that the Wards dismantle the shack. When they refused, Bell said he would be back—and that night, Bell convinced at least eleven of his friends from Creel City to force the Ward brothers out for good. Some accounts even said the mob was even bigger: some people claimed that twenty or thirty men had been on the scene to confront the two brothers.

They arrived at eleven o'clock, under the light of a full moon, armed with Winchester rifles. Six of the men approached the shack, while the other six stayed with the horses, fifty feet back from the shanty.

Inside, the two Ward brothers were talking with a third man named Elliott. Some say they were planning to move Frederick's shanty from the land that John Bell claimed, over to a claim that Charles held.

Bell pounded on the crooked door for some time. Eventually, Fred Ward opened the door.

He was promptly dragged off and beaten. Someone caught him by the collar and pulled him into the crowd, and then the mob dragged him around the corner of the building, where someone shot him in the back with a shotgun, and someone else shot him with a revolver.

Charlie yelled out into the darkness, asking his brother if he was okay.

The men outside fired their rifles at the shack.

Charlie came out of the shanty, shouting, "I give up!"

Before he could take another step, however, someone shot him in the neck—and when he fell face-down into the dirt, they fired two more bullets into his back.

Their friend Elliott left the shanty, too. He darted through the door and started to run, but the crowd caught him. They made him get down on his knees and beg for mercy. If he refused, they told him, he would die like the others.

While Elliott begged for his life, the crowd kicked and beat him. "Don't kill him," Major Uline said. "Let him run for it."

They watched him run for his life. Then the men took a final look at the Ward Brothers' bodies and headed home.

Later, John Bell tried to claim that his visit had been peaceful—and he blamed his compatriots for the shootings.

"I told them not to bring fire-arms," Bell told investigators later. "I did not wish trouble."

He didn't deny that he and his fellow land speculators had been at the scene when the Ward brothers were killed. His account of the story, however, is decidedly one-sided—considering that the Wards were outnumbered.

"I came up to the door," Bell told investigators. "I rapped and asked Ward if he was there, and I told him I wished him to come out and get off my claim. They were some time getting around. They made a good deal of noise in the house. The door was shut and seemed to be barred. We waited ten minutes, and thought we heard the pulling up a rifle.

"They opened the door quickly. Fred and two others rushed out.

"Fred Ward said, 'What is it, boys?'

"He raised his hand as though to strike, and struck me on the knuckles. He said: 'You __, I'll shoot you.'

"The men within the shack all started to shoot: at least there were five shots fired. I was not armed. Two shots passed over my head.

"One bullet caught McQueeny in the left arm. Shooting began on both sides. All seemed to scatter and someone said, 'Scatter out and shoot inside the shack.'

"I couldn't say who was armed or not armed; didn't see a revolver or shot-gun in the hands of anyone except Charles and Fred Ward. Fred Ward came around and met me and he pointed a revolver at me. I struck him in the body and knocked him back again three feet away. He was twelve feet from the shack, and dropped there. He walked out of the shack of his own account; no one pulled him out; I think they shot after he dropped. A few shots were fired after Ward fell; I do not know who fired nor at whom the fire was aimed."

W. H. Elliott, the man who visiting the Wards when the mob reached the shanty, told a different story.

"I was there when John Bell came down and talked. Bell said Ward was on his claim. Charles Ward thought his brother was on his own claim. Bell left while I was talking the team to the barn, and was absent about three-quarters of an hour.

"We had hardly dropped asleep when we heard a noise, and the Ward boys woke me up. In a few moments, a man knocked at the door and called. Ward asked, 'What do you want?' The reply was: 'Come down to move this shack.'

"When we opened the door I saw between twenty and thirty men. I could not distinguish faces. Someone pulled Fred Ward out of the door, and pulled him to the south of the shack, and I judge there were a dozen of them hammering him. When Charlie saw they were hammering Fred he drew a revolver and fired five shots.

"In the meantime they tried to pull me and Charlie Ward out. The shots were fired at the shanty before I left it, and about five minutes after Fred Ward was pulled out there were two squads of men, some on the north and some on the west side.

"I got three rods east of the shack, when a man told me to halt, and I stopped. Then a man came with a shotgun from the east and said, 'Let me get at him till I shoot.'

"The whole squad of them came up from the west. Someone told me to get up and get, and I got away."

The next day, twelve men arrested and taken to Fort Totten. When military authorities declined to receive them as prisoners, a judge set the bail at two thousand dollars each, and the Creel City syndicate posted bond for the men.

At first, the men bragged about the murders, calling it frontier justice in a clear case of claim jumping. Some even congratulated the men for their "peaceable actions." Two days later, their future seemed even brighter, when the railroad announced an agreement to buy the land they had rescued for twenty-five thousand dollars.

Some of the men decided to push their luck. They took turns submitting bills to Fred and Charlie's father, Dr. Edward P. Ward, for services performed in connection with the coroner's investigation.

Fifteen months later, when the men went to trial, the men weren't nearly so cocky.

Dr. Ward sent a heavy-hitting attorney from Chicago to work with prosecutors from Fargo and Grand Forks. They seemed to have an open-and-shut case, especially against two of the men in the gang. One of them, Bickham Lair, was a local newspaper editor. He had admitted that he dropped to a knee and carefully sighted before shooting Charlie Ward.

On June 24, 1883 Dr. Ward wrote to one of his supporters in North Dakota.

"My dear friend ... Many times in the midst of the many calls upon my time, have my thoughts been of that far away place where cruel, murderous hands deprived our loving and beloved sons of precious life and fond parents of the last motive for life. My poor wife is inconsolable. Her health is very poor and she is frightfully broken down, about as bad as at first. Will the fiends ever be brought to justice? What can the people of Dakota think of temporizing with such a crime under the name of 'manslaughter' when the testimony of the mob themselves is convicting of murder?"

The prosecutors were stunned when both men were acquitted. Mob rule had overturned the rule of law.

Defeated, they declined to proceed with their cases against the rest of the defendants. All the men who had attacked the Ward Brothers were freed—and they all went back to work as if nothing had happened.

In fact, they even tried to claim the land on which the Ward brothers had been killed.

Their father, Dr. Ward, fought them at every step, from the local land office in Devils Lake to the head of the federal Interior Department. In the only justice he would receive, in September 1885, Dr. Ward won the land on behalf of Charlie's widow and child.

The men who murdered the Ward brothers might have escaped the rule of justice on earth, but they haven't been so lucky in the spirit world.

In life, none of them ever slept well again. They suffered nightmares and poor health, the result of guilt and pangs of conscience. And in death, the members of the murderous gang seem to be consigned to a lasting march across the prairie, seeking to fill the void they left in the lives of the Ward brothers' family.

The Blizzard Ghost

Everyone in North Dakota knows that winter travel is never safe. In 1887, a young pioneer learned that lesson the hard way. Even now, she offers her story as a warning to others.

CAROLINE WALTERS KNEW that something wasn't right. For days, she had been fighting back an ominous sense of foreboding.

Her husband, Edward, told her not to worry.

"I'll be fine," he said, kissing her gently on the forehead. "I'm just going into town to pick up a few supplies. The sky is clear. You can see for yourself that there's not a cloud on the horizon."

The air was, in fact, as clear as she had ever seen it. It was sunny, and the contrast between the bright blue dome of the prairie sky over a blanket of white snow on the ground almost hurt her eyes.

Caroline watched as Edward pulled on his boots and buttoned his heavy winter coat. He even smiled and winked as he tugged a woolen cap over his head. "It's hardly cold enough for a hat," he said, "but I'll wear it if it will make you happy."

As he steered the horse and wagon out of the barnyard, headed toward Devils Lake, she wanted to cry out, to stop him, to call him back to the cozy two-bedroom farmhouse he had built for her—but that would be foolish, she told herself. He would be fine. One quick run into town? He'd be back in the morning. After all, Edward had made the trip a hundred times before, and she'd never thought anything of it.

Still, Caroline couldn't shake the sense of dread she felt deep inside.

She had been sick at heart for the last three days, ever since he first announced that he would head into town on Friday.

"Please," she had begged him. "Please, just wait until Monday. Stay home with me this weekend."

Edward didn't understand her concern.

"This isn't like you," he said. "You've always been fearless."

"I can't explain it," she answered, "but if you leave, I can't help feeling that I'll never see you alive again."

He chuckled at the thought.

"If it will make you happy," he said. "I'll make the trip and back in a single day. I won't stay overnight in town this time. I'll come back to you before bedtime, no matter what."

Caroline watched him ride away, then reluctantly turned to her chores.

As she milked the cow in the barn, she thought she sensed a movement near the doorway. Instinctively, she called out for their dog. Bandit usually followed her husband everywhere, but it was possible that he had tired of the walk to town, turned around, and come back to the farm.

When Caroline realized that there was no friendly rustle in response, no bounding, four-legged friend to keep her company, she felt even more frightened and alone.

In fact, her anxiety grew worse over the next few hours. All morning long, she continued to sense movements around her, just out of the corner her eye—but when she turned to look, she couldn't see anything out of the ordinary.

A young Indian woman walked by around noon, and Caroline waved. She was happy to see another living soul—happy, and reassured, because no native person would ever venture out across the prairie if there were even a hint of bad weather to come.

At three o'clock, however, as Caroline was checking on Bessie for the night, she noticed that the sky had turned from blue to gray, and a few heavy flakes of snow began to fall. They landed on her cheeks and eyelashes, and melted, like tears.

Caroline herself began to cry.

"Stop it," she told herself. "You're being ridiculous. A little snow is nothing to get alarmed about. There's no wind but a soft breeze. The air is still clear, and you can still see for miles in every direction."

The sound of her own voice, however, seemed to pierce the cold air around her. Chilled to the bone, she wrapped her shawl more tightly around her shoulders and hurried back into the house.

Caroline was too nervous to eat. The sun had set, and the flickering light of the fire cast ominous shadows all around the room.

The shadows reminded her of people she had once known—like her grandmother, who died not long after Caroline and Edward moved west. She saw visions of her long-lost childhood friend Alice, who had died of pneumonia at age fifteen. She recognized Sarah, her cousin who had died in childbirth.

They were all gone now, but now in the darkness of her loneliness and fear, the shadows seemed to be waving to her, beckoning her, reaching out to her. Oddly enough, she felt some comfort in their shadows, and she kept the fire blazing so that they could keep her company.

As the evening wore on, Caroline settled into her favorite rocker and tried to read. The words meant nothing to her, though. She would read, then re-read, the same page over and over again. And every few minutes, she would rise and rush to the window, hoping to catch sight of her husband driving up the road.

As she watched and waited, the soft breeze outside turned into a steady wind. More than once, it tricked her into thinking that she heard the sound of horses' hooves and the creaking turn of wagon wheels in the yard.

Before long, she gave up trying to read and moved her chair over to the window, where she could keep a constant eye on the swirling snow in the darkness outside.

The clock on the mantle ticked steadily on as the snow continued to fall, harder and harder against the windowpane. She could hear the icy flakes crunching as they hit the glass. A small drift began to pillow up against the outside windowsill.

As one hour ticked steadily into the next, Caroline realized that it anyone traveling tonight would himself be facing a growing mound of falling snow.

And yet, Edward had promised to return to her that night—and he was a man of his word.

At midnight, she opened her door to look outside, and realized that a wall of snow two feet deep had piled up outside the farmhouse. By two a.m., when the snow had reached a depth of three feet, she had convinced herself that her husband was almost certainly stuck somewhere on the road to their house. By four a.m., she was inconsolable with grief. And by six a.m., the minute the sky began to lighten with the sunrise, she strapped on her husband's snowshoes and set out, determined to rescue him from the storm that still blew across the prairie.

She didn't even bother to latch the door completely behind her. As she stepped away from the farmhouse, the door blew open, and snow began to drift inside, covering the carefully braided rag rug she had made for the hearth.

Just a few steps into the barnyard, she was blinded by a white cloud of blowing snow that made it impossible to see beyond her outstretched arm.

She knew where the road was, however, and she had a strong sense of direction, so she plowed on, into the storm, toward the husband she knew would be waiting for her.

She forced herself to maintain a sense of composure. The icy wind forced a few tears from her eyes, but they were tears of determination, not sadness. She would save her husband. She would find him, and bring him home. She would not let this weather take him from her.

She walked for an hour, then two, never feeling herself grow weak, and never feeling the cold taking over her body. She used her fear as a source of strength, transforming her sense of helplessness into a sense of action and resolve.

At last, she reached a sheltered area near a small grove of trees. A silhouetted figure waited for her there. The snow still blew, obscuring Caroline's vision, but she could tell that someone was waving her closer, welcoming her with outstretched arms.

Caroline's heart leapt with excitement and relief—but as she raced toward the figure, Caroline realized that she wasn't looking into the familiar face of her husband. Instead, she recognized a woman she hadn't expected to see again in this lifetime—her grandmother. Caroline blinked, and realized that her friend Alice was there, too, as well as her cousin Sarah.

They reached out to embrace her, just as Caroline's frozen body crumpled into the snow.

Caroline's husband, who had decided to wait out the storm in the safety of town, survived. But Caroline's terrible premonition that she would never again see him alive turned out to be true. She was the one who lost her life in the snow that morning.

A few days later, newspaper reports would recount her death.

Devil's Lake, Dakota, Feb. 9.—The body of Mrs. Edward Walters, who disappeared a few days since, has been found near Devil's Lake. Mr. Walters came to Devil's Lake from his farm last Friday, and the storm became so severe that he could not return. His wife became alarmed at his prolonged absence, and started to go to her nearest neighbors. Her body was discovered a short distance from the road upon the open prairie, partly covered by snow and only about a quarter of a mile from her own door. The snow about the spot where she lay indicated that she had walked about in a small circle for a long time.

Horn Cloud's Revenge

Tales of unrequited love are as old as time, but the story of a young woman named Julia and her would-be suitor Horn Cloud seems especially tragic—because it's so familiar. It's the troubling account of a young man who abuses the woman he purports to love. What sets this story apart, however, is the revelation of what happened to Horn Cloud after he died, when his actions had consequences he didn't expect.

JULIA HAD EVERYTHING to live for—along with a stalker who didn't want her to live with anyone but him.

She was a Métis girl from the Devils Lake area, a mixed-blood descendent of French-Canadian fur traders and their Dakota Indian wives. She grew up along the south shore of the lake, where her parents were well-known hunters and traders.

She spent her days like most of her Métis counterparts. When she was a child, her parents showered her with time, attention, and homemade toys—but the presents didn't spoil her. They actually made her sweeter. Her face was never clouded with sadness or anger. She always looked happy. She even had laugh lines at the corners of her eyes.

As a young woman, Julia fell in love with a man named No Water. He already had a wife, but to the people of that time and place, that wasn't an issue. She simply became No Water's second wife.

Julia spent the winter with No Water at the Standing Rock grounds near the border of North and South Dakota. On a gray, cold day in March, 1890, she started for home with No Water, his first wife, and their child. They weren't alone, however. As they set up camp on the first night of their journey, they realized that a man named Horn Cloud was following them.

Julia agreed to talk to him, and they walked several yards from the tipi that she and No Water's other wife had set up for the night. As a cold wind circled them and patches of snow crunched under their feet, Horn Cloud's eyes seemed to glint oddly in the gathering dark.

"I love you," he told Julia. "I can't live without you. Please, come back to Standing Rock and be my wife."

Julia looked for No Water, but he had gone hunting in a nearby grove of trees. She took a deep breath and tried to let Horn Cloud down gently.

"I'm sorry," she told Horn Cloud, "but no. I'm staying with No Water, and we're going back to Spirit Lake."

At first, Horn Cloud seemed to take the rejection like a man.

"Fair enough," he said. He smiled and reached out toward Julia. "Let's shake hands before we part for good."

He grasped her hand and held it with an intensity that frightened Julia.

She turned to leave—but Horn Cloud wasn't about to let her go. Without a word, he pulled his six-shooter from its holster and shot her in the back. Julia fell—and Horn Cloud shot her again, striking her in the arm, shattering the bone.

And then, still without a word, Horn Cloud turned and shot his horse. It could only mean that he was planning to kill himself, too.

When Julia's husband heard the gunshots, he came running. As he reached his fallen bride, Horn Cloud took careful aim and shot him, too.

No Water dropped to the ground, mortally wounded. Horn Cloud casually walked over to the fallen man and shot him a second time.

Finally, No Water went into the tipi, where Horn Cloud's first wife cowered with her child. He barely seemed to notice the young mother. Horn Cloud reloaded his gun—and then shot himself three times. With a groan, he collapsed and fell face down into the fire in the center of the tipi.

Horn Cloud's wife didn't wait around to watch him burn. Instead, she ran for help.

While surgeons had to amputate Julia's arm, they managed to remove the bullet from her back. She was maimed and scarred, but she made a full recovery and remarried a year later.

Horn Cloud, on the other hand, didn't recover from his suicidal moves—even after death. His spirit still moves among the trees where he shot Julia and her husband.

At first glance, Horn Cloud looks surprisingly strong and healthy. He's still lean and muscular, and his head is wrapped in a clean red scarf. He looks fine—until you see his hands, burned by his fall into the fire pit, and still wrapped in thick white bandages.

He's a ghost who can't use his hands. Because of his fatal last acts, he can't touch anyone, or hold anything. Instead, he's trapped in a helpless spirit form, and all he can do is watch the world go by.

The Virgin Feast

The people at Fort Totten treasured their young women. Anyone who suggested that they were impure was asking for trouble—often from the women themselves. In the late 1800s, several young women staged a traditional Virgin Feast to humiliate one of their detractors—Wamnuha, also known as Billy Squash.

WAMNUHA WAS A handsome young man who thought of himself as a lady's man. When a young woman named Lucy Provincial rejected his advances, he started spreading lies about her.

She was a loose woman, Billy said—and he had taken advantage of everything she had to offer.

It didn't take long for Billy's stories to get back to Lucy. She knew she had to act fast to protect her reputation.

She invited every girl she knew to a feast, and she scheduled the event for a ration day, when all of the Dakota people would be at the reservation.

She set up the feast in front of the commissary building, the most prominent spot of the agency grounds, and everyone came to watch.

Lucy invited ten young women to sit in a circle around a small oblong stone—the holy stone her people used in all their feasts and ceremonies. The stone was so sacred that the tribe called it "The Grandfather." Lucy stuck a knife into the ground beside the sacred stone, and started passing food to all the girls in the circle.

Dozens of observers stood around them, watching.

Billy was in the crowd, and the other young men taunted him, challenging him to stop Lucy's performance. He pretended not to notice.

When the girls finished eating, Lucy stood up and began to speak.

"Some of you have been talking about me," she said. "You've been spreading lies."

Then she threw down the gauntlet.

"If any man within the sound of my voice can say anything detrimental to me, you should say it now. Make it public. If you can prove your claim, I'll leave the fort and you can maintain your honor."

Billy laughed uneasily, and his friends tried to push him into the circle.

A young Dakota woman, photographed in 1908 by Edward S. Curtis.

Lucy repeated her announcement, and the other girls offered a similar challenge.

Billy, coerced by his friends, finally mustered enough courage to step forward and reach out his hand to Lucy. The girl plucked the knife out of the ground, seized Billy by the blanket, and tried to drag him into the circle of maidens.

Billy resisted, and she flourished the knife and insisted that he should tell his story, her eyes flashing and her tongue going at a rate that would have unnerved a bolder man than Billy Squash.

He continued to resist as Lucy dragged him forward to make his accusation. Finally, he slipped out of his blanket, leaving it in the hands of the enraged girl, and raced across the prairie.

Lucy was vindicated. From that point on, everyone who had seen the ceremony treated Billy with contempt.

There's a subtle energy in the spot where Lucy held her virgin feast. Her anger still permeates the air. Look closely, and you can see her, glaring, in a red dress that reaches past her knees, with leggings underneath. She stands with her arms crossed defiantly—and her resentment is as fresh today as it was all those years ago.

Billy Squash, however, is nowhere to be seen.

The Phantom Ship of Devils Lake

J. Morley Wyard was a tourist who spent a day at the Devils Lake Chautauqua festival in July, 1893. As he rode a steamship home across the lake that evening, he witnessed a stunning phenomenon that others had only hinted at in the past: the phantom ship of Devils Lake.

If you visit Devils Lake this summer, you might be able to see it for yourself. In the meantime, you can read Mr. Wyard's account, which was published in a local paper.

JULY SEVENTEENTH, THE closing day of the Chautauqua program, 1893, was a typical North Dakota summer day.

The Spirit Water could not have wooed its devotees more enchantingly.

It was just such a morning when even the least imaginative might expect to see sirens sporting in the pellucid depths, or mermaids embayed in some secluded nook coyly combing their tresses as their beauty was reflected from the silver mirror.

There was not a fleck of cloud upon the sky or a ripple on the lake. Overhead the gulls swept by. Around the boat the terns and loons merrily played their antics.

Along the shore the trees in summer beauty were reproduced upon the crystal surface. The glamor of the mirage was over all.

When the boat was well out in the center of the bay, suddenly there appeared on the southern shore, westward of the fort, what looked like the hull of a large vessel, without mast or spar or sail, and the color of new timber.

Motionless it lay, distinctly in view, apparently a half dozen miles away, until, as the boat drew nearer to the fort, the Pointe of Rocks intervened between the vessel and the vision, and the specter vanished.

The steamer waited only a few minutes at the fort, but on the return trip nothing could be seen where half an hour before the phantom had seemed so substantial—only the dark foliage of the trees contrasting with the brightness of the water.

But, far down the strait that separates Graham's Island from the southern shore, there appeared the glint of a sail that, emerging from the distant outlet, came more clearly into sight.

Though the air was breathless, the fairy craft swept along with wonderful rapidity, until it might have covered ten miles in about as many minutes.

Its rapid flight could be definitely measured. Upon the shore the taller trees were outlined against the sky, and the mystic yacht sped past them close under the land, until it, too, like the sail less and motionless hull of the earlier trip, disappeared at the boulder point near Fort Totten. All melted into air, like the baseless fabric of a vision.

The whole spectacle was so beautiful that it would be a pity to spoil the memory of it with the materiality of any scientific explanation.

The Day Jack Kenny Lost His Head

Even though Devils Lake was part of the Wild, Wild West, most people kept their body parts in one piece. On those rare occasions when heads rolled or limbs came loose, the severed items were carefully buried. In 1895, however, when a dog ran through the streets of Devils Lake with Jack Kenny's head in his mouth, everyone remembered that they'd neglected to keep their former neighbor together.

JACK KENNY HAD a pretty good head on his shoulders until he met Agnes Baldwin—a brash-looking, outspoken woman with red hair and green eyes.

She had an hourglass figure, and she dressed in the Gibson Girl style that was fashionable at the time. She wore long, mutton-sleeved gowns with ribbons and lace collars, with her hair piled loosely on her head. She also wore plenty of pink lipstick, and blush to set off her green eyes.

Jack was bewitched by Agnes's beauty—and he was more than a little surprised that she would be attracted to him. After all, he wasn't much to look at. He wasn't very tall, and he was bald, and he was a little bug-eyed. When he spoke, his voice cracked—but most of the time he hardly talked at all. Still, he had a house, and a job, and a little money in the bank, and he didn't mind spending some of it on her.

The two of them usually went out for the blue-plate dinner special at one of the hotels downtown. They enjoyed wagon rides and brief excursions to neighboring towns. Once in a while, they took in a performance at the opera house.

When Agnes started talking about marriage and family, though, Jack grew even more taciturn than usual. He might have been a quiet man, but he didn't like being openly pursued. He had some pride. What's more, he couldn't see himself settling down with Agnes, who tended to drink too much and talk too loud when they were together.

One night, Agnes issued an ultimatum.

"Marry me," she said, "or say goodbye. You'll never see me again."

Jack took one long look at the woman.

He didn't say a word.

Neither did Agnes. Enraged, she simply picked up a lamp and hit him over the head, fracturing his skull and killing him instantly. Without a backward look, she stepped over his body and slammed the door behind her.

During the subsequent murder trial, prosecutors exhumed the skull to prove where the fracture was located. Later, defense attorneys dug it up again to help prove their client's innocence—but in a bit of dirty dealing, the prosecutors stole the head away from them to keep them from using it in court.

One of the attorneys hid it in a closet and forgot about it—until his dog found it and ran down the street to show off his bone.

Agnes was jailed for a time, but women normally weren't locked up for long periods, so she paid for her crime and moved on.

Years later, some people said it was no coincidence that Jack Kenny's head just wouldn't go away quietly.

"He never did get a chance to speak up for himself before Agnes beaned him," they said.

Some even reported something even stranger.

When Jack Kenny's head was skull from the dog's maw, his mouth was open—wide open.

That's not the worst of it, though.

His jaw was moving, too, as if he was finally saying "no."

The Devils Lake Sea Serpent

While most people have heard of the Loch Ness monster in Scotland, almost no one knows that a similar creature has been spotted repeatedly in the waters of Devils Lake. Is it an optical illusion, raised by the mist or the blinding sun? Perhaps it's a figment of some observers' overworked imagination. Some even have suggested that the Devils Lake Sea Serpent is a long-lost breed of reptile—an ancient throwback to the days of the dinosaur.

ONE SUNNY EVENING, two Dakota men sat on the shores of Devils Lake, fishing, chatting about the weather and planning a hunting trip, when one of them idly thrust his knife into a huge log lying on the water's edge.

When the log lurched to the side, the men realized that it wasn't a log after all—but a giant serpent.

As it slid away, the scaly monster snapped down trees like twigs and dislodged boulders as if they were pebbles. Finally, the serpent reached the water's edge, slipped beneath the waves, and swam to the bottom of the lake.

A giant sea monster has slithered into similar accounts over the years, too. Some early residents reported seeing a serpent that was fifty feet long and covered with scales. They described how the water would rise and boil whenever he surfaced. Reportedly, he left a six-foot wake behind him when he swam away, and that he blew water out of his mouth like a man swimming. Some said he left the lake at night to sleep on land, and that he would leave a slimy, sticky trail when he crawled along the shore.

The most vivid description of the sea monster say he was eighty or ninety feet long, with green skin, ragged fins, bristling scales, alligator jaws, sharp, pointed teeth, white horns, and red eyes. He had a habit of coming to the surface at sunset, when the glare of the setting sun made his giant eyes look like they were on fire.

The serpent even appeared during the winter, when the lake was frozen. He would break through several feet of ice with his head, breathe deeply, survey the scenery, and search for game. When he caught a rabbit or a fox in his mighty jaws, he would swallow it whole in a single gulp.

A vintage illustration of historic sea monsters

Some people theorized that the serpent is a long-lost remnant of the dinosaur age. Some say he was caught in a giant glacier and dragged to the site. Others say he slipped in through a series of underwater tunnels and canals that snake under the North American continent, as far away as the Great Lakes. Some even say he stops a hole in the bottom of the lake with his tail.

According to one version of the story, the sea monster was actually responsible for the death off the Dakota warriors we met at the start of this book.

Originally, when the sea monster first appeared, Devils Lake was so polluted that all the fish disappeared. Little Shell, the chief, sent a medicine man named Ke-ask-ke (Big Liar) to investigate.

Ke-ask-ke found a band of Dakota Indians living on the shoreline. They had already beaten the Ojibwe in one battle, and they were planning another attack. Suddenly, a mystic spirit man named Owanda the Seer appeared in their midst. He warned them that if they continued to pursue their enemies, a huge monster would rise from the watery depths of the lake and destroy them all.

The Indians ignored the holy man. The warriors dressed for war, and they began to dance and drum and sing, along with the women and children of their village.

Just as they were about to go on the warpath, the earth began to tremble under their feet, and the lake began to rise and boil.

A giant sea serpent emerged from the water. His enormous eyes flashed like copper in the sun, while his enormous head moved from side to side. His short, powerful legs propelled him at incredible speed toward the shore.

The Indians fought for their lives, but the monster was too strong for them. One by one, he swallowed almost everyone in sight. Only a few managed to escape with their lives.

Within days, the lake water turned salty. The fish died, and the lake became unlivable.

Chief Little Shell convened a gathering of medicine men, and they danced, sang, and prayed for a solution. That's when their leader, Ma-che-gombe, announced that they would have to investigate the mystery firsthand. He commandeered the biggest boat he could find, and he insisted that the medicine men get in to row it out to the center of the lake.

As they rowed, they came to a choppy area of water, where large bubbles were rising to the surface.

The men panicked.

"Ma-che-gombe is crazy," they said, "to bring us face to face with the sea monster. We have no chance of overpowering him."

They wanted to throw Ma-che-gombe overboard, sacrificing his life to save their own. However, Ma-che-gambe convinced them they had nothing to fear.

Suddenly, the boat started spinning in a whirlpool, and one of the men went overboard. He went around and around, going deeper and deeper, until he disappeared.

"He's gone to the grave of the sea monster," they said.

That was enough. The men started sharpening their knives. It was time to kill Ma-che-gombe.

"Stop," Ma-che-gombe told them. "The holy man is the spirit of the water. The Great Spirit won't take him from us."

They rowed around the whirlpool until the holy man reappeared, thrown clear as if he'd been shot from a cannon. Then he described what he had discovered.

Deep in the water, he said, he had found a hole where the water came out boiling—the mouth of a subterranean passage that connected to an underground river. Just like the Mississippi River, he said, the underground waterway ran all the way to the Gulf of Mexico. When the sea monster made his way into Devils Lake, all the fish slipped into the underground stream, and they were never able to swim back into the lake.

The War Maiden

In the old days, it was unusual for Native American women to go to war—but not unheard of. Those who chose to fight were usually young girls who were the last of their line, or widows whose husbands had fallen in battle.

Not only could the women fight, but they also inspired their fellow fighting men to feats of bravery and daring. A storyteller Smoky Day once shared this story of a Dakota war maiden.

THERE ONCE WAS a chief named Tamakoche, who had three sons and a daughter named Makatah.

When his sons were killed in battle, he spent all his time with his daughter—and he spent most of that time praising the brave deeds of her brothers. He would chant war songs to her, and she would dance. That's how she came to love the thought of war.

As she grew into womanhood, she became one of the most sought-after beauties in the area. Makatah didn't care to marry, though. She had only two ambitions: to prove that she had the heart of a warrior, and to visit the graves of her brothers in enemy territory.

One of the men who asked for her hand was a young warrior named Red Horn. He gave her expensive gifts, and he encouraged influential members of the tribe to speak to her on his behalf. He even tried to use his father's position as a chief to force a decision in his favor.

A second man, Little Eagle, could only love her from afar. He was an orphan, poor and alone, and unproved as a warrior. He was so insignificant that nobody thought much about him, including Makatah.

One day, the village learned that the Cut-Head band of Dakota were planning to attack the Crows at the mouth of the Redwater, a tributary of the Missouri. Makatah asked her male cousins whether any of them expected to join the war party.

"Three of us will go," they replied.

"Let me go with you!" she begged. "I have a good horse, and I won't handicap you in battle. I only ask your protection in camp as your kinswoman and a maid of the war party.'

"'If our uncle Tamakoche sanctions it,' they replied, "we will be proud to have our cousin with us, to inspire us to brave deeds!'

The chief listened in silence as he filled his pipe, and seemed to think long and hard about his daughter's request. At last he spoke, with tears in his eyes.

"Daughter, I am an old man. My heart beats in my throat, and my old eyes cannot keep back the tears. My three sons, on whom I had placed all my hopes, are gone to a far country. You are the only child left to my old age, and you, too, are brave—as brave as any of your brothers. If you go I fear that you may not return to me, but I can't refuse you my permission."

The old man began to chant a war song, and some of his people, hearing him, came in to learn what was going on. He told them all, and immediately many young men volunteered for the war party, in order to have the honor of going with the daughter of their chief.

Each watched eagerly for an opportunity to ride at her side. At night, she pitched her little tipi within the circle of her cousins' campfires, and she slept without fear. Young men brought fresh venison to her every morning and evening.

On the third day of their expedition, scouts returned with word that the Crows were camping nearby. The band decided to attack the next morning at dawn. They agreed that in honor of her father, Makatah would lead the charge. As soon as the fighting began, however, she would be expected to drop back to a place of safety.

Makatah had no intention of falling back, but she didn't tell anyone what she had in mind.

That evening, the warriors sang war songs, vying with one another to tell brave tales of the battle to come. Red Horn was one of the most outspoken of the group. The lonely, unknown Little Eagle stayed silent.

Suddenly, all eyes turned to look at Makatah, as she came riding through the camp on a horse. She was wearing her father's war bonnet, and carrying the two war bonnets that had belonged to her brothers. Clearly, she planned to fight.

At daybreak, everyone mounted their horses and waited for the signal to attack—a single high-pitched yell, like the long howl of the gray wolf before he attacks. When at last the call came, five hundred warriors whooped in response. At the same moment, Makatah and her pony shot out in front of the group like an arrow.

Her white doeskin gown was trimmed with elk's teeth and ermine tails. Her long black hair hung loose, bound only with a strip of otter skin, and the eagle feathers on her war bonnet floated far behind. In her hand, she held a long coup-staff.

Makatah stayed with the warriors as they fought. As the battle progressed, many of them yelled, "Go back! Go back!" but she didn't listen.

The warriors fought a brave battle, but eventually, they found themselves on the losing side, and some began to retreat. Makatah tried to follow, but her pony was tired, and she fell further and further behind. Most of the men passed her as they fled, determined to save their own lives.

When Red Horn caught up to her, his pony was still fresh. He could have pulled her up behind him and carried her to safety, but he didn't even look at her as he galloped by. He had declared his love for her more loudly than any of the others, and now he had left her to die.

Just then, Little Eagle rode up to her, unhurt.

"Take my horse!' he said. "I'll stay here and fight!"

Makatah looked at him and shook her head, but he sprang to the ground and lifted her onto his horse. He swatted the horse's flank and sent him at full speed back to the Dakota camp. Then he took Makatah's tired horse and turned back to join the rear guard of fighters.

Before long, Little Eagle lay dead, killed in battle.

That night, as the Dakota gathered around their campfires, they began to name the fallen, and weep. They were stunned into silence when Makatah joined them there. She was a frightening sight: she had stripped of all her ornaments and torn the fringes off her dress. Her ankles were bare, her hair was cropped close to her neck, and she led a pony with its mane and tail cut short. She was in mourning.

Publicly, she declared herself the widow of Little Eagle, even though she had never been his wife. He had saved her life and her people's honor, she said. He was a true man.

The old warriors murmured in agreement, but the young men—all those who would have gladly taken Makatah as their wife—were embarrassed and ashamed.

The years passed. The War Maiden lived to be an old woman, but she remained true to her long lost love. She never married anyone else, and for the rest of her life she was known as the widow of the brave Little Eagle.

"You don't have to be a man to be a fighter," she would say, "and you don't have to be a wife to be a widow."

The Stairway to Hell

A few miles from Devils Lake, in a shelterbelt of trees near an abandoned farmstead, a mysterious outdoor stairwell leads to a dark, manmade cave. The steps are old and crumbling—and those who dare to follow them, beneath the surface of the earth, soon find themselves in a place that time forgot.

A STRANGE SILENCE surrounds the site that area residents call the "Stairway to Hell." Normally, the hush is broken only by the call of wild animals—but sometimes it's pierced by a bone-chilling scream.

The site gained some fame during the late 1990s, when national media outlets described its mysterious depths. I went there with my father, who has lived in Devils Lake for most of his life. We followed six steps down to an empty hollow in the ground, and what we saw was mind-boggling.

The chamber at the bottom of the stairs is hardly more than eight feet long, like a burial crypt. A small group of people could manage to fit inside—especially if they don't mind sharing an underground tomb with mice, spiders, or bats.

When the snow melts in the spring, or when the ground is saturated with heavy summer rains, standing pools of water collect at the foot the stairs. That might explain the musty smell that rises from its depths—but it doesn't explain the scent of sulfur and smoke that threaten to overwhelm some visitors.

The entire compartment is finished with hardened concrete and carved with dark, mysterious symbols. Some are Masonic: most people will recognize the traditional "G" with a compass, engraved over the entrance. Other engravings look like Hebrew letters or Egyptian hieroglyphs. A few etchings have worn and washed away with time

Most people believe that an immigrant farmer built the stairs—and the vault—by hand, back in the 1890s when he homesteaded the land. But why? No one knows. Some think it could have been used as a mikveh, or a ritual Jewish bath. Others believe it's a chamber for occult meditation and communion with spirits.

Some fear that a mysterious stairwell on an abandoned farmstead leads straight to Hell, as in this 1866 illustration by Paul Gustave Doré

It's those spirits, more than anything else, that seem to fill the void. Orbs of bright light, like flocks of birds, dart up and down the steps. Moving currents of air make some spots in the passage—which is already cool—bone-chillingly cold. The sound of breathing bounces off the walls, and a strange thumping noise seems to reverberate like the pounding of a heart.

While screams have only been reported sporadically, the subterranean whispers of the tomb are constant.

"Stay," the spirit voices mutter. "Stay."

The Haunted Train Station

The Devils Lake train station is a strange place to wait for a train. There, in the dead of night, lonely passengers often discover that they're not the only ones waiting for arrivals—or departures.

IN A CITY as isolated and remote as Devils Lake, train travel is still an efficient way to get to larger urban areas. Every night, one train rumbles in around midnight, heading east to Minneapolis. Just before dawn, a westbound train makes a stop on the way to Montana.

Meanwhile, the rest of the town is sound asleep.

The station itself is a small brick building. It was state of the art in 1908, but now it's somewhat worse for wear. In the summer, a warm breeze blows through the structure, carrying with it the sound of crickets chirping. In the winter, waves of cold air blast through the waiting area whenever the door opens. Even so, it's functional, and almost everyone in town has passed a few hours within its walls.

Late at night, the depot is unstaffed. The lobby doors are unlocked, so passengers can come and go as they wish. The police stop in periodically to make sure everything is peaceful.

It usually is. There's no television or internet on site, and often, there's no one else to talk to. The stationmaster sometimes leaves a portable radio playing on a shelf, broadcasting pop or country music—but most people simply turn it off and sit in silence.

That's when they notice a sound in the background that never goes away.

Call it the sound of ghosts, or spirits, or imprints of strong emotion, but the walls echo with the noise of a century of travelers. Breathe in, and you can even smell the leather of their bags. Close your eyes and you might be overcome by waves of sadness at the thousands of departures that have taken place at that spot—or sudden bursts of happiness, at the subsequent reunions.

Back during the 1940s, hundreds of brave young men gathered here at a single time, accompanied by family and friends determined to see them off. As a band played and women fought back tears, the young men boarded the train for a four-hundred mile journey to Fort Snelling, in Minneapolis, where they would be trained to fight in World War II.

Not surprisingly, some of the soldiers didn't come back—at least in corporeal form.

A turn-of-the-century postcard shows passengers and cargo ready to be loaded at the Great Northern Depot.

There are those who say the war ghosts are the most difficult to see. No matter how much time has passed, they still arrive sporadically, stepping off the train to search for the mothers and sweethearts who promised to meet them at the station. They walk inside the depot and pace the tile floors, watching and waiting for a reunion that never comes.

There are even a few older ghosts, of settlers and pioneers, who wait for their wives and children to join them on the new frontier.

Some stop in simply to see if their possessions have arrived at the station. Back when the rail line first reached the city, life got easier—and the population boomed. Until then, people, goods, and crops could only move by wagon or water, over prairie trails and along the Red River.

What's more, once the trains came, anyone with two nickels to rub together could order anything they wanted from the Sears Roebuck catalog, and it would be delivered within days.

During the 1870s, surveyors for the Northern Pacific Railroad started planning a route through North Dakota. Initially, they chose a path that would have taken the trains along a course a hundred miles south of the city, through Fargo and on to Bismarck. In 1878, however, the railroad magnate James J. Hill bought the St. Paul and Pacific Railroad and renamed it the "St. Paul, Minneapolis and

Manitoba." Hill wanted to skirt the Canadian border all the way to the Pacific Northwest, but the lure of mining fortunes in Montana shifted his route through the Devils Lake area. At Hill's insistence, the residents who were already in the area moved a few miles up from their previous town site, called Creel City, and the town of Devils Lake was born.

The happiest spirits at the train station are newlyweds, who took the train out of town for a once-in-a-lifetime honeymoon trip. They're joined by the vacationers who once rode an open-air train to the Chautauqua campgrounds, to hear celebrity speakers and spirited political debate.

Sometimes, however, death itself waited on the rails. Outside the station, the tracks are still haunted by the souls of travelers killed in a train crash a few miles east of Devils Lake. You'll meet them on the next page.

The Wreck of the Oriental Express

The Great Northern Oriental Express left St. Paul at 10 a.m. one Sunday in April 1907—but no one on board know that its final destination was less than a day away.

THE RIDE FROM Grand Forks to Devils Lake was like any other, that long, dark night of April 15, 1907. In the mail car, clerks sorted letters and parcels as the train rumbled down the track. A newsagent from St. Paul read the paper and chatted with the conductor. A Greek immigrant, who spoke very little English, nodded to his fellow passengers and smoked. Outside, the sky was black, with few stars to light the travelers' way.

The train had slowed down as it passed through small settlements in eastern North Dakota, ready to take on new boarders at isolated stops and stations. When it reached Bartlett at 1 a.m., it was rumbling along at thirty-five miles an hour.

Suddenly, the wheels began to squeak, as they lost their bearing on the track. Peter Ferguson, the engineer, tried desperately to stop the train, but without contact with the rails, the wheels merely spun.

Passengers rocked back and forth as the cars wobbled side to side and then, with a hideous screech, the train left the track completely and careened over a ten-foot embankment—still moving at more than thirty miles an hour.

Passengers were flung against shattered glass windows and over twisted metal seats. In the sleeper car, men and women were tossed from their beds. A few stragglers in the dining car were upended over tables and chairs, and riders in the observation car were thrown to the floor.

The cars at the front of the train were crushed. The mail car shot past the engine and exploded. A mail clerk named Harry Jones was killed, but his colleague, another clerk named Fodness, dove through the flames to carry his body out of the wreckage. The smoker car was crushed as it telescoped against the express car in front of it. The seats were torn from their moorings, burying passengers in a pile of twisted metal. One smoking passenger was killed instantly; only his feet were visible before flames consumed his body. The Greek traveler, who had a deep gash in his head and a severed left foot, was

Three passengers died and many were hurt in a train wreck east of Devils Lake.

also trapped; he was incinerated before rescuers could reach him. Within minutes, both the mail and the luggage cars were completely destroyed by fire.

In the countryside, people heard the crash four miles away. There were no highways or paved roads back then, so surgeons boarded a hastily called train car from Devils Lake, while another train left from the town of Michigan, carrying a coroner and several physicians.

Newspapers listed the injured that were treated at the scene, as well as those who were taken to area hospitals. Alfred Qualley, of Osgood, North Dakota, had internal injuries and crushed feet. A Mr. A. Saunders, of Clarence, Missouri, had a broken thigh. The train's fireman, Roy Curtis of Larimore, North Dakota, had a dislocated shoulder. The mail clerk who tried to save his colleague had a broken arm, burns on his head, and internal injuries. Matt Nelson, of Fossion, Minnesota, had a broken rib. J. A. Weeks, a travelling salesman from Minneapolis, twisted his knee. Ike McDowan, a travelling salesman from Grand Forks, North Dakota, was badly bruised, while the newsagent from St. Paul had a deep cut in his leg.

After an investigation, railway officials said the rails had been tampered with, and the tracks had been spread, in an attempt by miscreants to wreck the train. Others suspect that the company—or some of its employees—shortchanged maintenance and repairs on the track.

Today, there's nothing to mark the scene of the crash—except for the ghost of the Greek traveler who was pinned in the wreckage. If you watch carefully from the train as it passes through Bartlett, you might be able to catch a glimpse of him. He's balding, with heavy brows and a thick, graying beard. He still holds a hand-rolled cigarette, and its burning red ember marks the scene of his death.

The Ghosts at the Great Northern Hotel

The ghosts at the Great Northern can check out whenever they like—but at least one of them can never leave.

STEP AWAY FROM the train station in Devils Lake, cross the street, and you'll find yourself on the footsteps of the Great Northern Hotel—a local landmark that served as a way station for thousands of travelers over the year.

The Great Northern Hotel at the turn of the twentieth century. Notice the balcony in the foreground, where two U. S. presidents delivered speeches to crowds on the street below.

The Ghosts at the Great Northern Hotel   141

The Great Northern hotel lobby was an elegant gathering spot for travelers and area residents alike.

The impressive brick building went up in 1911. Franklin D. Roosevelt and Harry S Truman both rode the train into town, stepped off at the Great Northern Depot across the street, and delivered inspiring speeches from a balcony on the south side of the building.

More often, elegant women—in gowns, gloves, and feathered hats—met within is walls for tea and planned lavish socials on the site. Their husbands gathered for highballs and cigars in the parlor. They strolled across plush carpets and inlaid tile floors, danced in the grand ballroom, and gazed through windows hung with velvet curtains. Lovers trysted in the rooms upstairs, where railroad men could also stay—laying down seventy-five cents for a single room, or two dollars for a room with a bath.

Some, it would seem, have never checked out.

Today, the triangle-shaped building, which looks a little like the Flatiron building in New York City, has been renovated. The old hotel rooms are apartments now, and the gathering rooms on the main floor serve as offices.

The building is usually quiet—almost deathly so—except for unexpected sounds that manage to pass through from the Other Side.

Some residents notice the sound of children running through the hallways. Others hear whispers, as well as peals of distant laughter. It's not unusual to hear the soft strain of music echoing out from where the ballroom used to be, along with the clinking of glassware and the murmur of low conversation.

Spirits congregate most often where the reception desk used to stand, waiting for service that no longer meets their needs, and a bellman who never comes.

The ghosts can be seen, as well as heard. A few people have noticed a tall, thin man who looks almost real—except for the fact that he's translucent. He wears a bowler hat and a long overcoat, and he routinely walks through walls where doorways used to be.

Some people feel spirits settling next to them on their sofas, or sitting on the ends of their beds. Occasionally, a fast-moving ghost seems to bump into the residents in the hallway. Doorknobs turn, and doors slowly swing open by themselves. Drawers are often found ajar, and small articles of jewelry and clothing frequently go missing for days, before they reappear in places their owners wouldn't expect. There can even be electrical energy in the air, which leaves some people with a tingling sensation on their scalps or in their fingertips.

While most of the ghosts at the Great Northern are simply passing through, there is one who seems doomed to relive the worst days of her life. She's the spirit of young chambermaid who fell for the charms of a traveling salesman one night in the 1920s. He was nothing if not persuasive, and he managed to convince her to spend a night with him in his room.

By the time she realized she was pregnant, the salesman was long gone. Knowing that her reputation would be ruined, the young woman paced the halls for weeks before she ultimately killed herself.

Today she still paces the floors of the old Great Northern, crying quietly, and waiting in vain for the father of her child to step off the train across the street and check back into the hotel.

The Water Witch of the West

Water. It's one of life's most basic necessities. For pioneers on the North Dakota prairie, it was a constant, indispensable requirement—and when people needed it most, they turned to a railroad conductor named Eastman.

EASTMAN DIDN'T LOOK like a mystic. He was a railroad conductor, well into his fifties, with a gray beard and wrinkles, and he spent most of his time collecting tickets and keeping order on the train.

In his off hours, though, he was also a conductor of the metaphysical kind—and he had a gift for finding water where professional well diggers came up dry.

Eastman's tools were modest: he simply gathered a bundle of freshly cut willow branches, with the leaves and buds still on, and split them into V-shaped rods.

As merchants, farmers, and townspeople watched, he held the two ends of a branch in his hands, holding the pointed end of the stick straight up. Slowly, he would march across the prairie. The branch stayed upright for several yards, as the crowd trailed behind, observing every step.

Before long, the branch began to twist and turn in his hands, until it was sticking straight out, parallel with the ground. He slowed his pace and moved ahead, until the branch pointed straight down. That's when he would stop and make a mark in the grass with his heel.

Then he moved on, and slowly the branch would begin to rise, until it was pointing straight up again. "There is your water," he would say.

At one point, he explained his methodology for a magazine writer.

"Whatever kind of attraction there may be, I know it is there. I have located fifty wells along the railway without failure. I picked it up when I was a boy of thirteen, by watching an old blind Negro witch for water on my father's farm.

"Not everyone can succeed at it. There must be something in the theory of a magnetic current flowing between the operator and the hidden water through the medium of the green willow or the witch-hazel. I can't explain it, any more than I can tell you why one man succeeds at water-witching and another fails.

Eastman demonstrated his skill while on a break from his duties as a train conductor

"I have located a flowing well alongside five dry wells that had been located in the ordinary fashion. I must have found nearly five hundred good wells in the Dakotas, Montana and Idaho in the last twenty-five years. There isn't anything in it for me, and I have no reason for trying any Bunco games.

"Do I voluntarily twist the twigs? Not on your life. Grip one end, next my hand, and see if you can keep it from twisting, or take one end by yourself as we go back.

"There, what did I tell you? Of course, it twists of itself. Why, I have had my hands blister from the force with which the twigs pull down when there is water close to the surface. After you have located water, you must walk away from it until the twigs are upright again. The distance between the location and this other point will give you a rough estimate of the number of feet in depth you must dig before you are likely to strike water."

No one knows how many water sources Eastman actually discovered during his time away from the trains—or how many communities thrived and grew because of his contribution. Whenever you need a drink of fresh water on the prairie, though, a part of Eastman is there with you, wishing you well.

The Vision of White Thunder

You would think that being dead is a sad thing—but time after time, the ghosts in this book reveal that being dead is really just a state of mind.

A Dakota man named White Thunder first delivered that message during the 1800s, when he lived to tell about a near-death experience that lasted for hours. If you've ever read other stories about near-death and out-of-body experiences, you might be surprised at how well it dovetails with contemporary accounts.

Here it is, in White Thunder's own words—just as he told it when he was alive.

WHEN I WAS a young man I loved to go on the chase after buffaloes. I was fond of all kinds of hunting. When I was older I married my wife. Now I have two children and I do not care for the sports of my boyhood days. I often think of what our Holy Men tell us of the Happy Hunting Ground because the day will surely come when we shall all go there. I had often wished to know more about it.

One day my wishes were gratified. Now I know about the Happy Hunting Ground and about the change that we call death.

It came about in this way. My people were on the march. The Great Father at Washington had sent word to us that we must move to the Missouri River and that he would give us our food at that place. While we were on our way there our people camped on the banks of the Thunder Creek. That place was about three sleeps distant from the Missouri River. At night I lay down on some buffalo robes to rest. My wife was busy preparing our supper.

While I was resting I must have fallen fast asleep. When I awoke I saw two of my people standing near me. They wore white blankets. The white blanket is the sign of the Holy Lodge.

These men said to me, "Come with us."

I found that they spoke the language of my people, although they were strangers to me. I quickly sat up on the buffalo robes and they said again, "Come with us."

I supposed that Spotted Tail had sent for me to come to his tepee.

I told my wife I would go with these men, but would soon return. She did not hear me, so I spoke again. Again she did not hear me, so I arose to go to her.

As I did so I had a most curious sensation. My body seemed to be very light. It did not have any weight. I was as light as air. I moved over to my wife and spoke again. But she paid no attention to me. I could not understand it. It was the first time in my life that she had not heard me when I spoke to her.

I looked back at the place where I had been sleeping. There I saw another man lying where I had been resting. I went over to him and uncovered his face. Then I was still more surprised. I saw myself as I had been when I first lay down to rest.

I looked at my hands and my body. They were the same as the hands and body of the man on the robes.

I examined the man more thoroughly and found that he was dead. It was my body.

How could this thing be? I was as much alive as I had ever been and yet there were two bodies just alike, but the flesh-body was dead.

I then realized that I had two bodies, a flesh-body and a spirit-body. My wife could not see my spirit-body. Formerly I had been in that flesh-body all the time. Now I was out of the flesh body and yet I appeared just the same. I had often heard our Holy Men talk of such things, but I had not understood it as I did then.

My wife could not hear me talk now that I was outside my natural body. What should I do? She would soon come and try to awaken me. I could see her. She would think that White Thunder was dead. How could I tell her?

While I was thinking about it one of these men who was dressed in white said, "Come with us to the tepee of the Great Spirit. He has sent for you."

I went with them.

They said that they would lead the way to the land of the Great Spirit, the Happy Hunting Ground. They told me that they too once occupied bodies of flesh, just like the one lying there on those skins. They said that each of them at one time had carried about a body of flesh just as I had been doing. But now the body of flesh had gone back to the earth, just as my body would do in time. They told me that they would take me to the land of the Great Spirit and in a little while they would bring me back again to my earth-body. I must go back into it again and live for many winters.

Taking a last look at my wife and children, I departed from the earth with my guides.

As I went through the air I looked far off over the earth. As I looked, I saw many buffaloes, elk, deer, and other animals that had once inhabited that country.

My guides told me that whatever the Great Spirit once creates never dies. The Great Spirit had created my spirit-body. It would never die. Some time the body that I had fed on the earth would die and return to dust.

They said this was also true of animals. The Great Spirit gave each a spirit-body in the same shape as the natural body. As the spirit-body grew, the natural body also became larger; and when the time came for the natural body to die, the spirit-body passed out of it, just as I had passed out of my natural body. The spirit-body remained on the earth and the natural body went to decay. They told me that man could destroy the natural body of the animals, but he could not destroy the spirit-body. The spirit-body was the life of the natural body.

Soon we came to some very high mountains, much higher than any I had ever seen before. The guides said that all the mountains of the earth were once much higher than they now are. Through the eternal ages they had been sinking lower and lower. After a time they would become plains.

As we went on and on we lost sight of the earth. Before me I saw what looked like a great and shining river. It seemed to extend far up into the sky. I could not see the end of it. The guides said it led to the land of the Great Spirit. All the people that live on the earth and live good lives at last go away on that river. The river has no end, but flows on and on through the sky. There is no end of space; there is no place where it stops.

As we went up that river I saw that the banks were dark and gloomy. I asked the guides why that was. They told me that when we returned to the earth they would take me through those dark places, but not now. First they must take me to the Great Spirit of their people.

After a time it seemed as though the sun was rising. The banks of the great river were becoming lighter. Soon we approached the shore and saw the tepees of my people, saw friends whom I had formerly loved in the earth-life coming to greet me. I was overjoyed. They welcomed me to the land of the Great Spirit.

After I had rested with them for a time, I went with the guides to the Great Tipi, the home of the Great Spirit. He welcomed me. He told me that he had sent to the earth for me in order that I might learn the truth about the Spirit Land of the Dakotas. He wanted me to see it and to go back to the earth and tell my brothers what I had seen; tell them to treat all men as brothers, to be kind to those who were in sickness or suffering and then, when the time should come for everyone to leave the earth-body, all would be welcome in the land and in the home of the Great Spirit.

He said, "Now go, my brother, follow your guides and fear no danger."

When we went forth the guides showed me many strange places and conditions. I saw spirits who were happy. I saw those who were in sorrow. I saw those that had been bad men while they were in earth-life, and I saw those that had been murderers. All were suffering for the evil deeds they had done while they were in the flesh-body. I felt very sorry for them.

As we went on and on the regions became darker and darker. The guides said that we were passing through the dark places which we had seen along the shining river.

After a time we found ourselves back on the earth. The guides took me to the place where my people were camped on the Missouri River. I saw that my wife was sitting beside my body crying. My children were with her calling for their father.

As I looked at my flesh-body, wrapped as it was in buffalo skins, I dreaded to go back into it again. Now I did not have that load to carry about. I could move about without any effort. The guides said that I must go back. I seemed to fall asleep.

When I awoke I found myself again in my body. I looked through my natural eyes. Before, I had looked through the eyes of my-spirit-body. I groaned. I was in great pain. My hands and feet felt as though they had been sleeping. I struggled to get free. My wife cut the cords that bound my body and I sat up.

My wife and children cried for joy because I had come back to them. When I arose, I found that I had my heavy body to carry again.

Sister Saint Alfred's Deathbed Revelations

Most ghosts want to share the crowning achievement of their lives. For one ghost, however, that achievement occurred at the moment of death.

FIRE WAS A constant threat during the early days of Devils Lake. Most buildings were hastily constructed of wood, and pioneers relied on open flames for light and heat.

The Indian school at Fort Totten actually burned down twice: in 1883, the main buildings of the old Mission school were destroyed by fire. It was rebuilt, but it burned down a second time in 1926.

That was the fire that took Sister Saint Alfred's life.

For decades, the Indian schools had been operated by the Gray Nuns, an order of teachers and nurses from Montreal, Canada. Sister Saint Alfred, the school superior, had been in North Dakota for four years. She was sixty four.

"The fire," the *Devils Lake World* reported, "is believed to have started from a defective chimney flue. The school is a total loss, while the Catholic Church, which stood nearby, was also burned to the ground.

"One hundred Indian children of all ages set for other school children in the state a laudable example, when they marched in perfect order, half-dressed, into the snows outside with the temperature standing at ten above zero, without a single hitch or injury. The sixteen Catholic nuns in charge of the school were not required to issue a single command or reprimand as the children followed out orders of preceding fire drills."

Sister Saint Alfred, however, knew she couldn't live with herself if a single child had stayed behind. She escorted her staff and students out, and then she went back in to make sure that everyone had made it to safety.

When she didn't return, two other nuns went in and found her lying unconscious in the attic, close to death. The smoke had been too much for her. While she regained consciousness at the hospital, briefly, she didn't live long. Within days, she developed pneumonia and died.

The Sisters of Charity of Montreal, commonly known as the Grey Nuns of Montreal, were founded in 1738 by Saint Marguerite d'Youville, a young widow

Sister Saint Alfred died a heroic, selfless death. What she shared during her final hours, however, was nothing short of miraculous.

As she lingered in the twilight world between life and death, she had visions. She described seeing the Virgin Mary, as clear and lifelike as if the Mother of God had been standing next to the doctors and nurses who came in and out of her hospital room. She saw the infant Jesus, whose birth was being celebrated during that cold December week. The Christ child, as she described him, was lying in a wicker basket, wrapped in white swaddling cloth, so close at hand that Sister Saint Alfred thought she could reach out and touch him.

Her doctors and nurses didn't understand what Sister Saint Alfred was seeing. They thought she was mumbling a novena in a pneumonia-induced stupor.

"Most holy infant Jesus," she murmured, "true God and true man, our Savior and Redeemer; with all earnestness and respect, we beseech thee, by that charity, humility and bounty, which thou didst display in thy infancy, graciously undertaken for the love of us, that thou vouchsafe to grant us the favor we now beg, if it be for the honor of God and our salvation."

As the hours ticked away, she saw winged cherubs in her room, singing Christmas hymns to the sound of chapel bells.

And as her fever climbed and her breathing grew more shallow, she also felt herself beginning to grow younger, slipping out of her tired, old body, and returning to the slender form she had taken for granted when she was an eighteen-year-old novice.

At the time, she had started wearing a plain gold band to signify her marriage to Christ. Now, as she lay dying, she told visitors that she could feel herself rising from her bed, standing straight and tall, and wearing a floor-length gown of pure white silk.

A sheer silver veil replaced the peaked grey habit that normally framed her face, and her hair—long, dark, and thick—hung in two straight braids to her waist.

As the other nuns wept in the hallway outside her hospital room, Sister Saint Alfred began to sing. At first, they didn't recognize the word, but soon they realized that she was echoing the strains of *Ave Maria*.

The last thing Sister Saint Alfred saw in this life was a bright white light, illuminating the falling snow outside her window. For a moment, it filled the entire room. She recognized Jesus, now fully grown—and as he reached out to take her hand, Sister Saint Alfred died.

The Edwards House

Camp Grafton is a busy place. Every summer, it's inundated with National Guard troops. Some of the men you'll see there, however, aren't in the National Guard. They're fulfilling their own missions, even from beyond the grave.

CHRIS FROSAKER, A Norwegian immigrant who farmed and lived north of Sheyenne, North Dakota, looks like most of the men around Devils Lake.

He wears coveralls and a blue denim shirt, along with a black cap and wire-rimmed glasses. In the winter, he wears long johns under his clothes and a flannel shirt over them. His cheeks are chapped from too many years of sun, wind, snow, and cold, and he usually has a tin of snuff tucked into his back pocket.

Just one thing sets him apart: Christ Frosaker has been dead for years.

Frosaker was the stonemason who laid out the Edwards House, a local landmark at the National Guard camp near Devils Lake. If historical artifacts are any measure, it's probably the most haunted house in the state.

It's most recognizable ghost, however, is the man who built it.

When it was new, the Edwards House was a lonely sentinel on the outer edge of Camp Grafton. It was constructed of seven thousand stones—each one hand-cut to fit by Frosaker and his men, and each one a tangible reminder of thousands of years of history on the northern plains.

Construction began during the fall of 1938 and continued for two years. The house was part of a large Works Progress Administration project that also established a range of other camp structures, like mess halls, bathhouses, and a camp infirmary.

The stones were cut in the middle of winter. When temperatures dipped to record lows of twenty below zero for forty-one days, the cutting continued; Frosaker and his men simply put up a tent and kept working.

For many years, the building was known as "The Stone Cabin" or "The Governor's Cabin." In 1977, it was officially named "The Edwards House" in honor of Heber Edwards, who served as North Dakota's Adjutant General from 1937 until his death in 1962.

The house is remarkable in itself, but most of the furnishings and construction materials have a story of their own.

- The marble step at the front entrance came from the *Inter-Ocean*, the first newspaper in Devils Lake. Typesetters there would set type for their weekly editions on the stone.
- The lamps on either side of front entrance are from a horse-drawn vehicle that used to carry passengers from the train station to hotels.
- The log holders in the fireplace were forged from the rails of a narrow gauge railroad line that ran on the Fort Totten Military Reservation.
- The kerosene lanterns that hang from the ceiling were used in the Great Northern train depot.
- The anchor from Captain Edward E. Heerman's Steamer *Rock Island* hangs above the mantle. The steamer hauled the mail from Devils Lake to Fort Totten before the turn of the century, and it was named after the site upon which Camp Grafton is located.
- Some of the timbers and beams in the roof were fashioned from the telephone poles that carried the first long-distance voices into Devils Lake. Others came from a water tower that supplied water to steam locomotives.
- Some of the oak used to construct bunks, chairs, and couches came from old Army escort wagons. Some came from the hull of the *Minnie H*, the steamboat that carried passengers on the lake until 1908.

Ghosts can be tied to physical locations—either by choice, or out of habit. Some can be called back to any place that had special meaning for them. Others seem to leave an imprint there.

Most people would probably expect the artifacts in the house to be the draw for most ghosts. They look for the old typesetters from the pioneer newspaper to tap phantom letters into place, or for the lamps to flicker and glow, as if they were being carried through wind and snow outdoors.

Few people expect ordinary Christ Frosaker to stop by—and even fewer recognize him for the ghost that he is.

Still, his message echoes through the years: in the spirit world, material possessions are less important than the energy that went into their creation.

The Lost Tribe of Garske Colony

A small group of Jewish pioneers homesteaded in the Lake Region at the turn of the last century. Their settlement is long gone, but their cemetery remains—a windswept monument to dreams and disappointment on the prairie. Few people know it's there. Even fewer manage to visit it. And yet, a strange phenomenon has sprung up there over the last several years.

THE JEWISH SETTLERS who founded the Garske pioneer colony were once just as optimistic as the other settlers around them—and maybe even more so. Today you can find them near Highway 17, at the top of a windswept hill, in the Sons of Jacob Cemetery.

Simon Ettinger is buried there, twenty miles north of Devils Lake. A husband and father of five, he died in 1891, six short months after he won the title to his one hundred sixty-acre claim. He widow and children were left with land they couldn't farm, and ten dollars to their name.

Maier Calof is there, too. His wife, Rachel, documented their family's homesteading experience in her memoirs, *Rachel Calof's Story*.

Not far from Mr. Colof, you'll find Mandel Mill, who ran a little corner store in Devils Lake. He used to go door to door with a wagon full of fresh pike and walleye from Minnesota.

They were all part of the Garske Colony, a groundbreaking pioneer settlement that was established in the 1880s.

Like their new neighbors, they came from Europe. They had sailed across the Atlantic on overcrowded liners, with everything they owned bundled into wooden chests and barrels.

Almost everyone in North Dakota had fled poverty and oppression in their native lands, but the Jews had suffered more than most. They had come from Russia and Poland, where pogroms had been instituted to punish and eradicate their people. Roaming bands of soldiers and vigilante thugs moved through Jewish neighborhoods, looting homes and businesses, and beating any Jews who tried to defend themselves.

Rachel Calof, one of the Jewish settlers from the Garske Colony

In Europe, the Jews were merchants, because they hadn't been legally allowed to own land. In the United States, however, the government was giving land away to any man or woman who could rise to the challenge of cultivating it for future generations.

The Jews knew nothing about farming—but to people who had been given a second chance at life, the offer of free land and a fresh start, unfettered by oppression and persecution, seemed almost irresistible.

Between 1882 and the advent of World War I, more than eight hundred Jews filed land claims in North Dakota.

They were smart people. They had managed to survive through thousands of years of harassment. Certainly they could manage to grow a few crops on the rich, black fields of North Dakota.

How hard could it be?

They were about to find out.

Two of the earliest settlers in the Garske Colony were Morris Kohn and Herman Kaufmann, two brothers-in-law who came from Hungary in 1881 after a plague wiped out their vineyards. They started out with three hundred and eighty dollars, three horses, and a rickety wagon. One of the horses ran away, and a spilled can of kerosene caught fire and burned their tarpaper shack—along with a good portion of the prairie. They built a sod hut, instead, and planted forty acres of potatoes. When the farm failed, they both moved to Chicago.

Davis Rubin was another pioneer in the early days of the colony. At the end of his life, he recounted the experience.

I settled in 1892. I took a homestead and bought land (a quarter section). Got money from the Jewish Society of New York at six percent. We got money from the local banks at twelve percent and a bonus of ten percent, so can't wonder a Jew couldn't farm. The first Jewish settlement was founded by Baron de Hirsch. He was a millionaire and left money for these settlements. He built them homes and got them farming outfits, but most of them left in '88 or '89. There was no donations. When I come in 1892 all the colonial settlers left except three or four. Most of the Jews that came in the 90s made good. The colonial settlers had a rabbi and everything in the religious line. But there was very little improvement in the county and very little to do. When they threshed, they slept in the straw piles and drank slough water, and they decided most anything would be better than farming, so they left. The Jewish Relief would lend $500 to $800 on a quarter section of land. My home was in Overland Township, T. 857, R. 62, Section 30.

Pioneer life was hardest on the women, who were used to living in close-knit communities and cities with thousands of fellow Jews.

In North Dakota, they were isolated, hundreds of miles from their lifelong friends, families, temples, and traditions. The men farmed—and helped each other farm—which often meant that they would be out in the fields for days. The women languished in one-room shanties, with no one but their children to talk to for months on end.

There was nothing to do but work. The women straightened their shoulders and set out to recreate their Jewish customs on the prairie. They spoke in Hebrew and lit candles at sunset on Friday night, when they prayed and sang songs from their homeland.

Even in earthen dugouts and tarpaper shacks, they were meticulous in establishing kosher cooking areas, with separate sets of dishes, kitchen utensils, and cleaning supplies—so that meat and dairy products would never touch. They kept kosher, too, despite the fact that salted pork was the one source of protein that kept every other settler alive.

More often than not, they went without meat. It was almost impossible to find kosher beef on the prairie, because there weren't enough rabbis to supervise the butchering. Occasionally, Jewish butchers from Minneapolis or Saint Paul would ship kosher cuts to the settlement, but with no ice or refrigeration, the meat usually spoiled on the train.

While a few of the dead in the Sons of Jacob cemetery led rich, full lives, most of the graves belong to children. Some lived a few days. Some had a few years. Charlotte Greenberg, who died in 1906, was only four years old when she died.

Each small marker in the cemetery represents a tragedy, a story of grief and loss, and a testament to the unforgiving nature of the prairie.

The Jewish homesteaders were determined to preserve the memories of their dead. In 1885, they bought the land for the cemetery. They carved a few monuments from fieldstone, but most had no money for tombstones. Instead, they immortalized their lost children and loved ones by punching names and Hebrew inscriptions into sheets of galvanized tin.

Closer to Devils Lake, another attempt to establish a Jewish settlement was taking place at Stump Lake, which the Indians called Wamduska. In the winter of 1881, fifteen Jewish men staked adjoining claims and planned to break up one thousand, five hundred acres at the site. They expected the railroad to push through their settlement, which they named Adler. They built a three-story, forty-six-room hotel and tavern beside the lake, and they named it the Wamduska House. Stores, houses, saloons and a school also sprung up.

Sadly, the railroad chose a different route, and within a year, the Jews were forced to abandon their fledgling town. The impressive Wamduska House stood as a testament to the failed vision until it was demolished in 1954.

The Garske Colony near the Sons of Jacob Cemetery wasn't the first community to have Jewish settlers, but it was the only one that took root—at least for a time. Ultimately, ninety Jewish men and women filed claims in Ramsey County for quarter sections of land in the area. By 1912, the Garske Colony was the Northwest's oldest Jewish farming settlement.

Some of the Jews did learn to farm—and they farmed well. They had been born in cities, though, and the cities called them back. Some sold their land at a profit, and moved to Devils Lake, Grand Forks, and Fargo, where they set up shop in their more familiar roles as merchants and shopkeepers.

For a time, Jews in the Devils Lake area had a full communal life. They celebrated high holidays in the courthouse—so court dates weren't set until those holiday dates were scheduled. A rabbi from Grand Forks came every fall with provisions and to help prepare kosher meat for the oncoming winter.

Other Jews, however, boarded trains for Chicago and New York. By the mid-1920s, the Garske settlers had all moved away.

A farmer named Nick Kitsch bought the land around their cemetery. He cared for it until he died, and his descendants have maintained the practice in his place. Even now, they cut the grass, mend the fence, and keep the prairie trail clear for visitors.

For decades, no one visited the site. Hardly anyone knew it was there. Most people failed to notice it, because the tiny plot blends in with the miles of open fields that surround it.

In the past few years, however, a strange phenomenon has sprung up. Visitors from across the country have been making their way to the Sons of Jacob cemetery.

Local people come to pay their respects to former neighbors, who were both foreign and familiar. Jewish people also feel compelled to visit the site. Some have distant relatives buried there. Others simply want to stand at the graves and pray.

In 2006, a collective of out-of-town Jews and Devils Lake residents rededicated the cemetery. During the ceremonies, they unveiled a marker with the names of a hundred and four settlers who once homesteaded the Garske Colony.

Today, at the Sons of Jacob cemetery, pebbles continually appear on the main granite monument, as well as individual graves.

The practice of leaving stones on a gravesite is a longstanding Jewish tradition. At one time, grave monuments were mounds of stones. Visitors added small pebbles to the mounds as a sign of respect and remembrance.

The tradition might date back to the days when ancient shepherds would keep a daily count of their sheep by tallying pebbles into a sling. Pebbles on a grave are one way of asking God to keep the souls of the departed in his keeping.

Eastern European Jews like those in the Garske Colony also placed stones on graves for superstitious reasons. Many of them believed that the souls of the dead lingered in their graves, which could lead to hauntings. The stones were one small measure to ensure that those souls would stay where they belonged.

The pebbles seem to accumulate at an astonishing rate. On balance, it hardly seems possible that visitors are bringing them to the site. Weeks go by when no one visits, and yet the pebbles continue to accrue, month after month, season after season. For a time, local people would even take the pebbles off the grave markers, not recognizing their significance—and yet, more and more stones are stacked there, every day.

There's no earthly explanation, but someone, somehow, is working to ensure that the children of Israel—especially those who belonged to the lost tribe of Garske Colony—are not forgotten.

The Ghost of the *Minnie H*

You don't usually expect to meet a sea captain plying his trade 1,500 miles from the nearest ocean—but one sailor, Captain Edward E. Heerman, was able to claim the inland sea of Devils Lake as his own for decades.

These days, Captain Heerman's steamboat voyages are a thing of the past. No one alive remembers them. But if you look closely, you might be able to spot Captain Heerman himself, still waiting for passengers on the ghost ship Minnie H.

IN LIFE, CAPTAIN Edward Edson Heerman looked as if he could have stepped out of a storybook. He was bearded, like all sea captains should be, and he smoked a pipe. He was perpetually sunburned, and when he walked, he leaned, as though he was braced for waves or wind.

Like so many settlers, Captain Heerman had traveled a long way to reach Devils Lake. He was born in Vermont in 1834. His parents were farmers who raised sheep, spun wool, and wove it into cloth. His family moved to Iowa when he was still a boy. At the age of sixteen, he left home and headed for the Mississippi, determined to seek his fortune on the great waterway of America.

He found it. By nineteen, he commanded his own steamboat, and a few years later he owned a fleet of thirteen riverboats that ran along the Mississippi and Chippewa rivers.

As railroads competed with riverboats for passengers and freight in the central corridor of the country, Captain Heerman started to look for new waters to explore. He headed west toward Dakota Territory.

In 1858, he helped establish a town along the Red River, near Fargo. During the Indian Uprising of 1862, however, the settlement was burned to the ground, and his expansion plans were put on hold.

In 1882, he made a trip to Devils Lake.

"Devils Lake was a beautiful body of water fringed with timber," he wrote in his memoirs. "The locality was dotted with other beautiful lakes. I examined the soil and believed I had found an empire of undeveloped resources."

Captain Edward Heerman and his daughter, Minnie

He sold everything he owned and moved to North Dakota, where he practically dragged a steamboat, piece by piece, thirty five miles across open prairie. He shipped fourteen train cars full of boat-building materials—including a sawmill and a boiler—to the end of the rail line in Larimore. He hired teams of men and horses to drag everything the rest of the way, through snow so deep that one of the loads was lost and never recovered. He built the ship in the dead of winter, in temperatures that reached fifty below zero.

Captain Heerman was also a family man, and almost all of his ships were named for his only daughter, Minnietta. The ship he built during that winter of 1882, the *Minnie H*, would be the most successful of them all.

Captain Heerman designed the *Minnie H* to carry freight, mail, and passengers from the train depot to settlements on the lake, including Fort Totten and the town of Minnewaukan. He did a booming business for almost thirty years.

During that time, however, Captain Heerman kept a record of the lake's water level. Each year, the lake grew smaller—until finally, his steamboat business receded, too.

The Minnie H *on Devils Lake*

In the fall of 1889, the *Minnie H* made her last trip to Devils Lake. The water level had dropped so much that the boats had to land at the narrows of the bay, a mile and a half from Devils Lake, and they were never able to get back to town again.

Captain Heerman turned the *Minnie H* pilothouse into a playhouse for his grandchildren and retired. He died in 1929, at the age of ninety five.

Despite the fact that he's been dead for decades, everyone in Devils Lake knows where to find his ghost. His place in history is marked by a boulder on a long-lost shoreline.

That boulder, in turn, is in the front yard of the school that was named for his ship: Minnie H Elementary, on the west side of town. That's where Heerman's passengers used to board the paddlewheel for a two-hour ride across the lake.

These days, when the youngest students see him, some think he's a crossing guard, patrolling the crosswalk in front of the school. Others mistake him for a kindly neighbor, enjoying a morning stroll.

Every now and then he stands up and stretches. He walks through the school building, past the classrooms, and out the back door. Then he heads northeast across the playground, and up the hill that leads to the railroad station—just in case there are travelers at the depot, waiting for a ride.

The ancient Greeks and Romans used to believe that the souls of the dead were ferried across the River Styx, the mythological river that separated the land of the living from the land of the dead. They buried their loved ones with a coin or two, so they could pay their fare across the water.

In death, Captain Heerman has stepped into the role of ferryman, conducting souls from one phase of life to another. Given his love of Devils Lake and her people, it's not hard to imagine him, still collecting coins and passengers for transport from one side of the lake to another—or from their earthly existence to a new life on the Other Side.

The Earl of Caithness

Like a doomed character from a Shakespearean tragedy, the short life of a Scottish nobleman still plays itself out on the prairie south of Devils Lake.

JOHN SINCLAIR SEEMED like any other rancher during the boom times on the Dakota plains—but the cultured, soft-spoken immigrant wasn't like any of his neighbors.

In fact, John Sinclair had a secret identity: he was the Earl of Caithness, Lord Berriedale of Scotland, and Baronet of Nova Scotia.

The Earl of Caithness was a true, honest-to-God nobleman. In his native land, he had the respect of royalty, churchmen, and the aristocracy—but to stay in Scotland, he declared, would be the death of his soul. He decided, instead, that his true purpose in life was to farm, to shepherd the land, and to invest his money and his spirit in the open, untilled soil near Devils Lake.

The aristocratic Sinclair came to the United States at the turn of the twentieth century, after spending nine years in Canada with the Bank of Montreal. When he moved to Nelson County, North Dakota, he was twenty seven years old. Before long, he had amassed a three-thousand-acre ranch south of Devils Lake. He named it after one of his titles: Berriedale.

He planted half of his land with wheat, barley, flax, and millet, and he brought in a dozen men from Scotland to work the crops. In the spring, he used thirty mules for planting, pulling four-gang plows—and he built a platform on his grainery so he could supervise his field hands

His dairy operation produced about fifty pounds of butter a day. Most of it was packed in two- and five-pound containers and shipped to Montana. He sold the rest, door to door, in Lakota.

Sinclair's neighbors knew he was cultured, but no one suspected he was royalty. He delivered milk and butter personally to his local customers, and when he headed into town he would usually stop at his neighbors' houses to see if they needed anything. During harvest time, he drove his buckboard into the fields to bring home-cooked meals to his crews.

John Sinclair, the seventeenth Earl of Caithness

John Sinclair could trace his family back to the year 875. At one time, his family's estate had been immense: the first Earl of Caithness owned the entire north of Scotland, from sea to sea, including the Orkney Islands.

Over several generations, however, the land had been subdivided among dozens of heirs—and while Sinclair eventually inherited the title, he didn't inherit any land to go with it. He had to be satisfied with impressive titles. He was Lord Berriedale from 1889 to 1891. When his father died in 1891, he also inherited the title of twelfth Baronet Sinclair of Canisbay, County Caithness, as well as the seventeenth Earl of Caithness.

Sinclair stayed on his North Dakota farm until 1905, when he was called home to Scotland to make improvements to his family's estate in Aberdeenshire. In 1910, he inherited the Castle of Auchmacoy and other property in Aberdeenshire. The inheritance also came with an income of twenty-five-thousand dollars a year.

The money was enough for him to move back to America and live in quiet comfort at the Hotel Balboa in Los Angeles. He passed his days strolling the streets of the upper-class neighborhood, and enjoying the sun and surf along the Pacific Ocean.

Only two people there knew his secret identity. One of them was Corridan H. Putnam, a mining engineer.

"He held all the titles as dross and preferred to live as one of the plain people of earth," Putnam said, after Sinclair's death. "His life was devoted to good works."

He also explained the reason for Sinclair's secrecy when it came to his royal stature. The motto of the House of Caithness, Putnam said, was "Commit thy work to God."

Unfortunately, Sinclair wouldn't be able to enjoy his fortune for long.

One day in May 1914, John Sinclair was a passenger on a Pacific Electric train. He was riding a local route that took people to the beach. The engineers were inexperienced, and they crashed into another train.

Several people were mutilated; newspaper reports at the time described body parts strewn along the tracks, along with a cacophony of screams and wails from the wounded.

At first, Sinclair's own injuries seemed relatively minor. His leg was hurt, but his doctors and nurses expected him to recover within a few months.

They were wrong. John Sinclair never walked again, and he never recovered from the shock of the accident, either. A year later, almost to the day, he died.

He was only fifty-six. After a modest funeral, he was buried at Forest Lawn.

While John Sinclair had power and privilege, his happiest years were spent on his North Dakota ranch. As he lay injured—first in a hospital, and later in a nursing home—he used to dream about his days at Berriedale, when he could walk through fields of ripening grain and ride thoroughbred horses across the prairie.

More than anything, he missed the stars and the Northern Lights.

When John Sinclair was alive, he used to walk outside at night, watching the stars. They were the same stars he watched from the luxury liner that sailed him across the Atlantic Ocean, and they were the same stars he could see from Scotland, or Canada, or California.

In North Dakota, however, the stars seemed closer, brighter, and more intense. They glittered against the backdrop of the Northern Lights—a celestial rainbow of red, green, yellow, and blue. They even fell from the sky, in summertime meteor showers that illuminated the darkest nights.

In primitive cultures, people believe that the stars are the spirits of the dead.

For the Earl of Caithness, who had a thousand years of ancestors breathing down his neck in Scotland, North Dakota offered an escape. It was one place on earth where he could be his own man, without the starry-eyed spirits of his ancestors pressing in on him from all sides, pushing their way into his everyday life, and shifting the way that other people saw him.

On the North Dakota prairie, he could chart his own course, shed his own light, and determine his own destiny. He could see life on his own terms—especially after dark.

After his death, the North Dakota prairie was a starting point for his own journey into the heavens. From his ranch, he could float among the stars, no longer weighed down by the expectations of his family or the weight of his titles.

That's why he lingers in those fields still, keeping his eyes on the heavens while his soul wanders the earth.

Queen Victoria's Maid

The Earl of Caithness wasn't the only regal settler on the prairie. In fact, one of Queen Victoria's maids made the shocking decision to leave Buckingham Palace in 1887, to live with her true love in North Dakota. The Milwaukee Journal published an article about her in September 1930. This is the story.

ROLLA, N. D.—For eight years Mrs. Harry Williams served as maid in waiting to Queen Victoria of England. Then she came to make her home in a log cabin on the windswept Dakota prairie. Now, at 76, looking back on it all, she is still glad that she made the choice.

And back of it all lies a most unusual love story—the story of a young English girl who gave up a life amid luxury with European royalty to suffer hardships in a pioneer section of America with the man she loved.

From the royal palace of England to the Dakota cabin was a long step—especially in 1887, when settlers were scarce and homesteaders had to undergo all of the hardships of pioneer life. But Mrs. Williams, who made the step because the man she loved had made it, has never regretted it: and today she and her husband agree that she chose wisely.

Mrs. Williams grew up in London as Marie Downing, an apprentice girl in a sewing shop. Becoming maid in waiting to Queen Victoria, she speedily became a favorite with the queen and was her personal attendant for years.

Several times the queen "loaned" the girl to the Empress Eugenie of France, whom she befriended when the Emperor Napoleon III was dethroned, and the young woman traveled over Europe with the deposed empress. The former empress' popularity was not great in those days, and in many places the populace was hostile to her; and for this reason Marie Downing, dressed in the empress' clothing, often rode in the royal coach, while the empress went disguised as the maid.

After the death of the Prince Imperial, son of Eugenie, she accompanied the empress to Africa to recover the young man's body.

It was in 1882 that Harry Williams—then a young man and the maid in waiting's sweetheart—came to America. He begged her to follow him and she planned to do so, but Queen Victoria induced her to stay in England for a while. The queen gave the girl a number of gifts, including some diamonds which she promptly sold so as to get money with which she and Harry Williams could buy land in the western United States. the queen also gave her a timepiece—originally as a rebuke for tardiness, but later she gave her an ornamental cast to put it in, and it is now one of the prized decorations on Mrs. Williams' mantelpiece in her little three-room home here.

Finally, after two years Queen Victoria consented to have her maid in waiting leave her service and go to America to join her lover. Her majesty presented her with trunks packed with linens, lacey silks and gowns worn by herself, and with a set of sterling silver tableware as well. The girl brought these with her.

At length, having crossed the ocean and half of the American continent, the girl got off a train at Minnewaukan, N. D., in midwinter, to be met there by Williams. They were married at once, and then, in an open sleigh drawn by one horse more than 100 miles, in weather that was below zero, to the site of their new home.

When they got there, the bride found that their log cabin was not yet complete, and they had to stay at a neighbor's home for a time. Mrs. Williams was ready for a pioneer's life—as she often did more than others, by mowing 100 tons of hay unaided, or by stacking large bundles pitched to her by her husband.

After returning from a trip to England in 1909, Mr. and Mrs. Williams leased their farm and bought a rooming house here. They were able to buy more silver, and they served their guests with sterling silver given them by Queen Victoria. More recently, they have been living alone.

Dressed in the gown in which she last served Queen Victoria almost half a century ago—a basque with a draped skirt of silk—Mrs. Williams loves to display her treasures to her friends. She has gowns, silver, silks, and other mementoes given her by Victoria, including a paper weight made of black marble just like that used in the tomb of Prince Albert.

Her most prized possession is a seal ring which the queen gave her. It has two Ms and two Ds, inverted, engraved on a green stone. Mrs. Williams explains that her majesty designed this ring for her so that she could re-address the queen's mail when needed: secrecy was imperative in state and foreign communications and that the unusual ring was used to seal the envelopes.

Victoria's Maid Tells of Romance That Brought Her to Cabin in U. S.

Faced Pioneer Life on Dakota Prairie

Castle to Plains

Above is a close-up of Mrs. Harry Williams as she appears today at her North Dakota home. At the left she is shown wearing the gown she wore when she last served Queen Victoria as maid in waiting. At the right, an old photograph of her as she appeared when she accompanied Empress Eugenie of France on a trip through Europe.

Rolla, N. D.—For eight years Mrs. Harry Williams served as maid in waiting to Queen Victoria of England. Then she came to make her home in a log cabin on the wind swept Dakota prairie. Now, at 76, looking back on it all, she is still glad that she made the choice.

And back of it all lies a most unusual love story—the story of a young English girl who gave up a life amid luxury with European royalty to suffer hardships in a pioneer section of American with the man she loved.

From the royal palace of England to the Dakota cabin was a long step—especially in 1887, when settlers were scarce and homesteaders had to undergo all of the hardships of pioneer life. But Mrs. Williams, who made the step because the man she loved had made it, has never regretted it; and today she and her husband agree that she chose wisely.

Became Queen's Favorite

Mrs. Williams grew up in London as Marie Downing, an apprentice girl in a sewing shop. Becoming maid in waiting to Queen Victoria, she speedily became a favorite with the queen and was her personal attendant for years.

Several times the queen "loaned" the girl to the Empress Eugenie of France, whom she befriended when the Emperor Napoleon III was dethroned, and the young woman traveled over Europe with the deposed empress. The former empress' popularity was not great in those days, and in many places the populace was hostile to her; and for this reason Marie Downing, dressed in the empress' clothing, often rode in the royal coach, while the empress went disguised as the maid.

After the death of the Prince Imperial, son of Eugenie, she accompanied the empress to A___ ___ ___ cover the young man's b___

Her Odd Romance

It was in 1882 that Harry W____ ___—then a young man and ___ maid in waiting's sweetheart—came to America. He begged her to ___ ___ ___ and she planned to do so but Queen Victoria induced her to stay in England for a while. The queen gave the girl a number of gif___ ___ ___ some diamonds which she promptly sold so as to get money w___ which she and Harry Williams could buy land in the western United States. The queen also gave her a timepiece—originally as a rebuke for tardiness, but later she gave her an ornamental case to put it in, and it is now one of the prized decorations on Mrs. Williams' mantelpiece in her little three-room home here.

Finally, after two years Queen Victoria consented to have her maid in waiting leave her service and go to America to join her lover. Her majesty presented her with trunks packed with linens, lace, silks and gowns worn by herself, and with a set of sterling silver tableware as well. The girl brought these with her.

At length, having crossed the ocean and half of the American continent, the girl got off a train at M___ ___ ___kan, N. D. in mid-winter to be met there by Williams. The___ were married at once, and then, ___ ___ ___ sleigh drawn by one horse ___ ___ ___ 100 miles, in weather that was far below zero, to the site of their future home.

When they got there the ___ ___ found that their log cabin was ___ ___ yet completed, and they had ___ ___ at a neighbor's home for ___ ___ ___ Mrs. Williams was read ___ ___ ___ neer's life—as she often ___ ___ ___ er, by mowing 100 tons o ___ ___ ___ unaided, or by stackin ___ ___ ___ bundles pitched to her ___ ___ band.

After returning fron ___ ___ ___ England in 1909, Mr. a___ ___ ___ liams leased their farm ___ ___ ___ a rooming house here. ___ ___ ___ able to buy more silv ___ ___ ___ served their guests with ___ ___ as ___ sterling silver given th___ ___ ___ Victoria. More recentl ___ ___ ___ been living alone.

Has Queen's Mementos

Dressed in the gown ___ ___ ___ last served Queen Vic ___ ___ ___ half a century ago—a ___ ___ ___ basque with a draped ___ ___ ___ silk—Mrs. Williams loves to display her treasures to her friends. She has gowns, silver, silks and other mementoes given her by Victoria, including a paper weight made of black marble just like that used in the tomb of Prince Albert.

Her most prized possession is a seal ring which the queen gave her. It has two Ms and two Ds inverted, engraved on a green stone. Mrs. Williams explains that her majesty designed this ring for her so that she could re-address the queen's mail when need of secrecy was imperative in state and foreign communications and that the unusual ring was used to seal the envelopes.

The Odd Fellows Dance Hall

Where do ghosts go to dance? They head for the oldest dance hall in Devils Lake, a second-floor site of revelry that withstood the great fire of 1884.

THE OLDEST BUILDING in downtown Devils Lake is a two-story social hall, constructed by soldiers who needed a place to convene in private life. Their days had been filled by drills and patrols—but their nights were filled with dancing.

When the Devils Lake Lodge of the International Order of Odd Fellows was formed in 1879, its members met in a vacant mess hall at Fort Totten. Seven soldiers chartered the group, and a special deputy grand master rode the train from Jamestown to Fort Totten to help get the local assembly off the ground. Some of the memorabilia from their first meetings—ribbons, badges, and organizational forms—is still on display in the fort's history exhibit. When you stroll through it, you can practically hear the murmur of their distant conversations, the echoes of their long-ago laughter, and the scent of cigar or pipe smoke.

Back in 1884, when the military closed the post, the former soldiers wanted a place to gather—so they built a new meeting hall on Kelly Avenue in Devils Lake.

At the time, Devils Lake had just experienced its first boom cycle of expansion and development. The train tracks had reached the depot on the south side of town, and enthusiastic businessmen and construction workers built sixty-five wood-frame structures in just four weeks.

The buildings were crowded together and cheaply made. When a stable caught fire in 1884, the entire business district burned to the ground. The Odd Fellows' Hall was the only structure to survive the blaze.

From the outside, the building still looks almost as it did when it was first built. It's a two-story brick structure, with arched windows on the front and a historic Coca-Cola advertisement painted on the north wall.

Inside, a creaky old staircase leads to the second floor. The stairs seem to rise forever. One by one they lead, higher and higher, to a long-lost past.

A nineteenth-century poster from the Independent Order of Odd Fellows

A century ago, the second floor of the Odd Fellows Hall was a dance floor. Some of the men had offices in the back, but most of the space was dedicated to music and dancing.

On long winter nights, a four-piece band would play into the early hours of the morning. Men would drink, young women would dance with their boyfriends, and children would sleep on a bench piled high with winter coats and furs. The old building can be a drafty, chilly place, but when it was crowded with dancers, the windows would fog up.

During the 1950s, the top half of the building was converted to apartments. Plasterboard walls went up to subdivide each unit, and artificial ceilings lowered the height of the rooms. Above the false ceiling and underneath the wall-to-wall carpeting, however, the bones of the dance floor remained, including six-inch floorboards of solid oak, and hundreds of pressed-tin ceiling tiles, each embossed with the patterned seal of the I.O.O.F.

Legend has it that the origins of fraternal societies date back to the exile of the Israelites from Babylon in 587 B.C., when tradesmen banded together for mutual support and defense. By the thirteenth century, their guilds were established and prosperous. During the fourteenth century, guild masters moved to protect their power and income by restricting access to the guilds. In response, the less-experienced "fellows" set up their own rival organizations. Smaller towns and villages didn't have enough men from the same trade to set up local guilds, so craftsmen banded together to form guilds for an odd assortment of trades—the Odd Fellows. Some records indicate that the first Order of Odd Fellows was established in 1452, by knights who met in London.

The Odd Fellows offered a universal moral code to its followers. Members were expected to believe in a Supreme Being, creator and preserver of the universe. They were encouraged to accept all men as brothers, and to offer sympathy, service, and support to those in need. They were held to high standards of friendship, love, and truth. In short, they were determined to demonstrate the difference between right and wrong.

They also believed in an afterlife; eternal brotherhood was a cornerstone of their community.

As the founders grew older and fraternities fell out of favor, the Odd Fellows eventually moved out of the building. For a time, it housed a café. For many years, it served as a clinic. After that, it was the headquarters of a law firm.

Most people who worked there locked the doors tight at sunset—because that's when the noises usually start on the second floor. On some evenings, mysterious, unseen visitors can be heard walking up the stairs, making their way to the second floor, and the floors above the office space thud with the sound of dancing feet. Distant strains of music filter through the air, along with the murmur of conversation, muffled laughter, and the clink of glasses.

Some say there's a logical explanation for the noises. There are apartments upstairs, and renters come and go. The building next door is filled with tenants, too. There's even a bar across the street, and hard-drinking men and women sometimes stagger past the Odd Fellows hall, laughing and shouting as they teeter on to their next destination.

But the noises continue well into the night, long after renters have gone to bed, well after the neighborhood bars have closed.

The sounds continue even now. Once a nightspot, always a nightspot—and the Odd Fellows Hall is clearly a clubhouse for ghosts.

Buffalo Bones

In Dakota Territory, no animal had a larger soul than the buffalo—and no animals gave more, suffered more, and died in greater numbers than the herds of bison who used to roam the land around Devils Lake. Like the rest of the ghosts of Devils Lake, they want their story told, too.

OUT ON THE open prairie around Devils Lake, you'll often see dust devils—small swirling clouds that rise up from dry fields and glide across the landscape. They move like a herd of animals, one following another, chasing their way toward the horizon. From a distance, you could almost confuse them for the spirits of the bison—heavy in life, but now lighter than air.

The buffalo herds in North Dakota were once the stuff of legend. Even when they were at their prime, most Americans couldn't imagine the huge numbers of animals that roamed the open prairie.

Charles Cavileer was one of pioneers who tried to describe the herds. He was crossing the prairie near Devils Lake when he was caught in an 1860s buffalo stampede. Luckily, he wasn't traveling alone: he was part of a wagon train, and there was safety in numbers.

At first, he reported, the oncoming buffalo looked like a black cloud on the horizon. The travelers pulled their carts into a two concentric rings—one on the outside, and one on the inside. In the center of the circle, Cavileer and his companions braced themselves for an onslaught.

They heard a low rumble as the bison approached. The rumble became a roar, and the earth shook, but when the herd reached the wagons the giant animals parted and swerved on either side, tipping just a few of the outside wagons in the process.

Cavileer and his fellow travelers could hardly believe the size of the herd. They sat in their circle of wagons for a full twenty-four hours as thousands of bison ran steadily past.

Later, they noticed that the bison hadn't just trampled the prairie lands in their path; their pounding hooves had stripped every last inch of vegetation from the ground, in a swath several miles wide.

Early explorers, of course, made the most of the buffalo as a source of food and clothing. The herds still prospered, because the Indians killed only what they needed to survive.

A pile of buffalo bones on the shore of Devils Lake, with the Minnie H *steamboat in the background*

As the region became more settled, however, hunters and tourists followed, hoping to claim a prize buffalo trophy for themselves. They killed the bison for sport, not survival, and often left most of the slaughtered beasts to rot in the sun. Some shot them from moving trains, and some riflemen bragged of killing seventy five to a hundred bison a day.

The trains themselves were a hazard to the buffalo. Every fall, flying sparks from the railroad would start prairie fires. L. C. Ives, a cavalryman with the Second Minnesota Volunteers, was returning from an expedition when he noticed the carnage that resulted.

"Plains burned in every direction," he wrote, "and blind buffalo seen every moment wandering about. The poor beasts have all the hair singed off; even the skin in many places is shriveled up and terribly burned, and their eyes are swollen and closed fast.... In one spot we found a whole herd lying dead. The fire having passed only yesterday, these animals were still good and fresh, and many of them exceedingly fat.... At sunset we arrived at the Indian camp, having made an extraordinary day's ride, and seen an incredible number of dead and dying, blind, lame, singed, and roasted buffalo. The fire raged all night."

On the shores of Devils Lake, buffalo bones piled up for years, bleaching white in the sun, until Captain Heerman and his men stacked them on his steamboat and ferried them to destinations back east. Sugar manufacturers could use the bones in a refining process, and factory owners paid eight to ten dollars for a railcar load.

For years, no one seemed to calculate the huge numbers of bison that were disappearing. The focus was on farming, not wildlife management. Within a generation, the herds were gone, almost as if they had simply vanished in the night.

During the 1800s, the wild buffalo were nearly hunted into extinction. Today, however, people are working to bring the mighty creatures back to life. Today, if you make your way out to the nature preserve at Sully's Hill, you can see new herds of buffalo, roaming at will through the fields and forest. Some farmers in the region have also started raising buffalo for food.

If you stand quietly enough on the prairie, you can sense more than just the movement of the animals: you can sense the presence of history, in the form of an entire group of animal spirits. The move in unison, traveling together as one.

They're huge, and heavy, and they lumber slowly when they walk, pressing against the surface of the prairie. They're as large as life, and they identify closely with the earth itself—even though the herd has thinned.

The Devils Lake Ghost Tour

If you would like to see the Ghosts of Devils Lake for yourself, be sure to visit the following locations. For a complete guide to area attractions, stop by the Chamber of Commerce and Tourism offices on Highway 2.

The Lake Region Heritage Center

502 Fourth Street, Devils Lake

Lillian Wineman's room is on the second floor of the old post office, which in itself is an impressive example of classical revival architecture. You can also look for the ghost of Charles Sneesby in the vintage federal courtroom, complete with an elevated judge's desk, gleaming wood railings, and wooden witness stand. Don't miss the detailed Native American display of dance regalia, artifacts, and information on the Dakota Sioux, and peek into a model tipi. See a reproduction of the *Minnie H* steamboat that carried thousands of passengers to the shores where Chautauqua was held. If you're a genealogist or researcher, visit the Daisy Hermanson Room, which houses hundreds of books filled with newspaper articles, pictures, and primary documents.

The Sheriff's House Museum

420 Sixth Street, Devils Lake

Get a taste for life at the turn of the last century in the Sheriff's House—a colonial revival home with two front parlors, a state-of-the art kitchen and dining rooms, and five bedrooms. The house is filled with original furnishings and belongings from the Lake Region's early days.

Historic Buildings

Take a walking tour of downtown Devils Lake, and you'll see dozens of remarkable buildings listed on the National Historic Register. Be sure to look for:

- The Old Main Cafe, at 416 Fourth Street. Upstairs, you can see a replica of Devils Lake's early Main Street, as well as photos that feature early street scenes from neighboring towns.
- The Wineman family's Opera House at 402 Fourth Street.
- The Great Northern Hotel at 201 Fourth Avenue.

- The train station across the street from the Great Northern Hotel at 350 Railroad Avenue.
- The I.O.O.F. hall, the oldest brick building in downtown Devils Lake, at 411 Fourth Avenue. Look for the vintage Coca-Cola mural painted on the north side of the building.
- The Masonic Temple at 403 Sixth Street.
- The old Carnegie Library at 623 Fourth Avenue.
- The Episcopal Church of the Advent—also known as the old Stone Church— at 501 Sixth Street East.
- The former high school—now Central Middle School— at 325 Seventh Street. If you have relatives that grew up in Devils Lake, you can probably find their senior portraits in the class photos that line the hallways of the second floor. They date from 1910 through the 1990s.

The Chautauqua Gallery

Lake Region State College, 1801 College Drive N

Stop by the Chautauqua Gallery at Lake Region State College and sample the cultural movement that swept the whole country during the late 1800s. For two weeks each summer, vacationers enjoyed popular speakers and presentations that both entertained and educated young and old alike. Some of the performers included Native Americans, who impressed their neighbors with elaborate displays of dancing, beadwork, and costumes. The gallery has a permanent display of memorabilia, and the library has a thirty-minute slide show with images from the festivals that were held on the shores of Devils Lake from 1892 to 1929.

The Devils Lake Cemetery

Fourteenth Avenue NE, between Seventh and Tenth Streets

Visit the mortal remains of many of Devils Lake's most famous—and infamous—residents at the sprawling cemetery grounds. Look for the towering monument to the Grand Army of the Republic, as well as the graves of Civil War veterans nearby.

The Lake Region Library

The city's public library houses a Scandinavian Section, a North Dakota Heritage Room, a George Johnson Genealogical Section, and microfilm copies of local newspapers.

Sully's Hill National Game Preserve

Take Highway 20 south of town, until it becomes Highway 57, and follow the signs. You can drive the four-mile car tour, looking for buffalo and stopping midway along the overlook loop. A nature trail hike will take you a mile and a half along a wooded stream and through forested hills. You can also hike to the lookout tower at the top of Sully's Hill.

Fort Totten Historic Site

417 Cavalry Circle, Fort Totten

Fort Totten Square, also known as Calvary Square, looks like it did when Fort Totten was a Civil War outpost. Start your tour at the Interpretive Center, and then visit Plummer's Store and the traveling exhibits. You can also take your pick of four self-guided tours that will let you follow four historical figures through a typical day in history. Continue around the square, and explore the Pioneer Daughters' Museum, which is filled with interesting artifacts and collectibles.

If you arrive on the right day in July, you can also reserve a spot for dinner at the Totten Trail Historic Inn. From there, attend the musical production at Fort Totten Little Theater. Complete your time travel with a room at the Totten Trail Historic Inn Bed and Breakfast. You'll sleep in the same rooms that once housed the fort's officers and their families. The rooms have been decorated to represent the era from 1870 to 1910.

Pioneer Daughter's Museum

Lake Region Pioneer Daughter's Museum, inside the Fort Totten Historic Site, is filled with artifacts from the early days of the fort—including uniforms and a collection of Michael Vetter's letters. The museum is staffed daily from mid-May to mid-September.

Fort Totten Days

The Spirit Lake Nation's annual pow wow, known as Fort Totten Days, is usually held during the last weekend in July. The event, which is open to the public, celebrates Indian heritage through dance competitions and exhibitions, songs, parades, Indian games, softball tournaments, a rodeo, and a run.

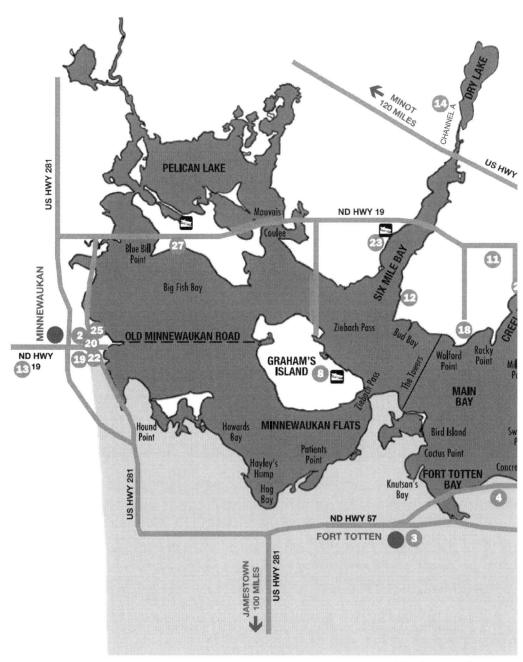

Bait Shops
1. Ed's Bait Shop
2. JJ's Bait Shop

Information Centers
? Devils Lake Visitor Center & Chamber of Commerce

▲ Minnie H Rest Area

Lake Region Points of Interest
3. Fort Totten State Historic Site, Museum & Little Theater
4. Sullys Hill National Game Preserve
5. Creel Bay Golf Course
6. Camp Grafton National Guard Camp
7. Lakewood Bible Camp

State Campground
8. Graham's Island State Park

Private Campgrounds, Cabins,
10. Ackerman Acres
11. Angler's Inn
12. Bayview Resort
13. Country RV
14. Dry Lake Campground
15. Eagle Bend Campground

The Devils Lake Ghost Tour

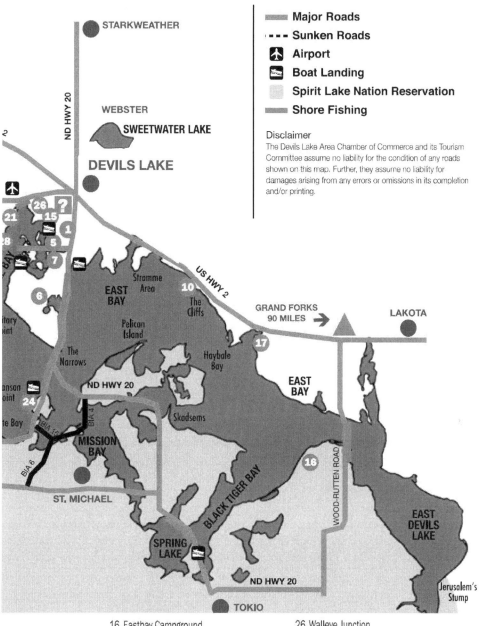

Lodges & Resorts

16. Eastbay Campground
17. Haybale Heights
18. Lakeview Lodge
19. McQuoid Outdoors
20. Perch Eyes Guide Service
21. Peterson Woods
22. Reel'm Inn
23. Six Mile Bay Campground
24. Spirit Lake Casino & Resort
25. Spirit Water Inn Resort
26. Walleye Junction
27. West Bay Resort
28. Woodland Resort

Map ©Transcript Publishing, New Rockford, N.D.
Used with permission.

Sources

The Legend of Minnewaukan
Rena Percival, "The Legend of Minnewaukan," *Devils Lake Illustrated* (Grand Forks, ND: Press of Grand Forks Herald, 1898)

The Ghostly Legend of Devils Lake
Brennan, Mary E., "The Legend of Minnewaukan—Mysterious Water" in *Collections of the State Historical Society of North Dakota, Volume 1* (Bismarck, ND: State Historical Society of North Dakota, 1906)

Burlin, Natalie Curtis, The Indians' Book: An Offering by the American Indians of Indian lore, Musical and Narrative, to Form a Record of the Songs and Legends of their Race (New York: Harper and Brothers, 1907)

The Song of Howastena
Collections of the State Historical Society of North Dakota, Volume 1 (Bismarck, ND: State Historical Society of North Dakota, 1906)

Introduction/History
The Early History of the Devils Lake Country (Larimore, ND: Printed by H. V. Arnold, 1920)

Robinson, Elwyn B., *History of North Dakota* (Lincoln, NE: The University of Nebraska Press, 1966)

Sumnicht, Mrs. G. H. et al., *A Bicentennial History of Devils Lake, North Dakota* (Devils Lake, ND: The Devils Lake Bicentennial Heritage Committee, 1976)

Wills, Bernt Lloyd, *North Dakota: The Northern Prairie State* (Ann Arbor, MI: Printed by Edwards Brothers, Inc., 1963)

The Museum Ghost
Scheer, Robert, "Collected Artifacts Many Years: Devils Lake Woman Found Indian History Was Right At Her Doorstep," *Minot Daily News,* October 24, 1964

Wilcox, Eleanor, "Pioneer Lil Wineman Remembers," *Devils Lake Journal*, July 1983

Officer Sneesby's Last Patrol
"Night Policeman Sneesby Shot Deat at Midnight by Bandits," *The Devils Lake World*, June 25, 1924

"Policeman C. R. Sneesby Lays Down Life in Protecting Life and Property of Community," *The Devils Lake World*, July 2, 1924

"Goldie Nolan Is First N.D. Man to Alcatraz Prison," *The Devils Lake World*, January 3, 1934

The Lightman at the Opera House
"Opera Houses" (Fargo, ND: Prairie Public Radio *Dakota Datebook*, February 18, 2004)

The Maiden on the Cliff
Davis, Jim, "Indian Legend" (Fargo, ND: Prairie Public Radio *Dakota Datebook*, October 27, 2008)

The Ghost Wife
Crow Dog, Leonard, oral storyteller, told in 1968

Federal Writers' Project in Nebraska, *Indian Ghost Legends,* Number Twelve (Lincoln, NE: 1937)

The Haunting of Mary Berri Chapman
"Hansbrough-Chapman" (Wedding announcement, *The New York Times,* August 17, 1897)

Hinman, Ida, *The Washington Sketch Book: A Society Souvenir* (Washington, D. C.: Hartman & Cadick, Printers,1895)

Stedman, Edmund Clarence, ed., *An American Anthology, 1787–1900* (Boston: Houghton Mifflin Company, 1900)

Duncan Graham's Island
Andreas' 1884 Historical Atlas of Dakota, as quoted by officials of Ramsey County, North Dakota at http://www.co.ramsey.nd.us/history.htm

"Biographies of Early Settlers on Graham's Island: Captain Duncan Graham," *Collections of the State Historical Society of North Dakota, Volume 3* (Bismarck, ND: State Historical Society of North Dakota, 1910)

"Duncan Graham" (Fargo, ND: Prairie Public Radio *Dakota Datebook*, December 5, 2008)

The Resurrection of Little Flower
McLaughlin, Marie L., *Myths and Legends of the Sioux* (Bismarck, ND: Bismarck Tribune Co., 1916)

Yellowstone Vic
Smith, Victor Grant and Jeanette Prodgers, *The Champion Buffalo Hunter: The Frontier Memoirs of Yellowstone Vic Smith* (Falcon Press Publishing Company, 1997)

The Story of Brave Bear
Collections of the State Historical Society of North Dakota, Volume 3 (Bismarck, ND: State Historical Society of North Dakota, 1910)

Holley, Frances Chamberlain, *Once Their Home; or, Our Legacy from the Dahkotahs* (Chicago: Donohue & Henneberry, 1890)

Garcia, Louis, Dakota Researcher and Honorary Tribal Historian, Tokio, North Dakota

Little Crow and the Indian Uprising
Berghold, Alexander, The Indians' Revenge, or Days of Horror: Some Appalling Events in the History of the Sioux (San Francisco: P. J. Thomas, Printer,1891)

Garcia, Louis, et al., *The History and Culture of the Mni Wakan Oyate (Spirit Lake Nation)* (Bismarck, N.D.: North Dakota Department of Public Instruction, 1997)

Alfred Sully's Game of Chance

Andreas' 1884 Historical Atlas of Dakota, as quoted by officials of Ramsey County, North Dakota at http://www.co.ramsey.nd.us/history.htm

Fiske, Frank Bennett, *The Taming of the Sioux* (Bismarck, ND: Bismarck Tribune, 1917)

Smith, Roderick A., A History of Dickinson County, Iowa, Together with an Account of The Spirit Lake Massacre, and the Indian Troubles on the Northwestern Frontier (Des Moines: The Kenyon Printing and Manufacturing Company, 1902)

Sully, Langdon *No Tears for the General: The Life of Alfred Sully, 1821-1879* (Palo Alto, CA: American West Publishing Company, 1974)

Workers of the Federal Writers Project of the Works Progress Administration for the State of North Dakota, *North Dakota: A Guide to the Northern Prairie State* (Bismarck, ND: State Historical Society of North Dakota, 1938)

Haunted Fort Totten

Andreas' 1884 Historical Atlas of Dakota, as quoted by officials of Ramsey County, North Dakota at http://www.co.ramsey.nd.us/history.htm

Mattson, Jack, et al., *Living History* Field Day Brochure (Fort Totten, ND: Fort Totten State Historic Site Foundation, 2005)

Nelson, Vance, and Bev Horne and Olivia Kingree, *Living History* Field Day Brochure. (Fort Totten, ND: Fort Totten State Historic Site Foundation, 2002)

Remele, Larry, *Fort Totten: Military Post and Indian School* (Bismarck: State Historical Society of North Dakota, 1986)

The Ghost of Pierre Bottineau

Minnesota Historical Society, St. Paul, Minnesota

Pierre Bottineau, Red Lake County Historical Society, Red Lake Falls, MN

The Story of Brave Bear

Holley, Frances Chamberlain, *Once Their Home; or, Our Legacy from the Dahkotahs* (Chicago: Donohue & Henneberry, 1890)

The Grief of the Only One's Wife

Holley, Frances Chamberlain, *Once Their Home; or, Our Legacy from the Dahkotahs* (Chicago: Donohue & Henneberry, 1890)

The Men who Fell with Custer

Eriksmoen, Curt, "Reno Blamed for Custer's Fall," *Bismarck Tribune*, September 20, 2008

Russell, Jerry L., *1876 Facts About Custer and the Battle of the Little Big Horn*, (Mason City, IA: Da Capo Press, 1999)

The Soldiers on the Staircase

Mattson, Jack, et al., (Fort Totten, ND: Fort Totten State Historic Site Foundation, 2004)

Dear Brother: Michael Vetter's Letters

"Dakota Cowboy Soldier," (Fargo, ND: Prairie Public Radio *Dakota Datebook,* January 13, 2006)

Moore, Rex, editor. *The Cowboy Soldier.* (Fort Totten, ND: Devils Lake Sioux Manufacturing Corporation, 1979)

The Haunted Little Theatre

Brennan, Mary E., "The First School at Fort Totten" in *Collections of the State Historical Society of North Dakota, Volume 3* (Bismarck, ND: State Historical Society of North Dakota, 1910)

Friends of Fort Totten, *Totten Trail Historic Inn: History* (Fort Totten, ND: Friends of Fort Totten, 2005)

Mattson, Jack, et al., *Living History* Field Day Brochure (Fort Totten, ND: Fort Totten State Historic Site Foundation, 2004)

Little Fish and the Indians of Fort Totten

Diedrich, Mark, *Mni Wakan Oyate: A History of the Sisituwan, Wahpeton, Pabaksa, and other Dakota that Settled at Spirit Lake, North Dakota* (Fort Totten, ND: Cankdeska Cikana Community College Publishing, 2007)

Garcia, Louis, et al., *The History and Culture of the Mni Wakan Oyate (Spirit Lake Nation)* (Bismarck, ND: North Dakota Department of Public Instruction, 1997)

Ignatius Court and the Indian School

Brennan, Mary E., "The First School at Fort Totten" in *Collections of the State Historical Society of North Dakota, Volume 3* (Bismarck, ND: State Historical Society of North Dakota, 1910)

Friends of Fort Totten, *Totten Trail Historic Inn: History* (Fort Totten, ND: Friends of Fort Totten, 2005)

Mattson, Jack, et al., *Living History* Field Day Brochure (Fort Totten, ND: Fort Totten State Historic Site Foundation, 2004)

Rain in the Face

Eastman, Charles A., *Indian Heroes and Great Chieftains* (Boston: Little, Brown, and Company, 1918)

Mrs. Faribault's Fresh-Baked Bread

Holley, Frances Chamberlain, *Once Their Home; or, Our Legacy from the Dahkotahs* (Chicago: Donohue & Henneberry, 1890)

Stallard, Patricia Y., *Glittering Misery: Dependents of the Indian Fighting Army* (San Rafael, CA: Presidio Press, 1978)

The Ghost of Grand Harbor

The Early History of the Devils Lake Country (Larimore, ND: Printed by H. V. Arnold, 1920)

The Guardian of the Grand Army of the Republic

Bolda, Den, *Grand Army of the Republic Monument* (http://heritagerenewal.org/stone/dlgar.htm)

Phisterer, Frederick. *New York in the War of the Rebellion*, 3rd ed. (Albany: J. B. Lyon Company, 1912)

The Union army: a history of military affairs in the loyal states, 1861-65 — records of the regiments in the Union army — cyclopedia of battles — memoirs of commanders and soldiers. Volume II. (Madison, WI: Federal Pub. Co., 1908)

The Devil's Heart

Eastman, Charles A., *Indian Boyhood* (Boston: Little, Brown, and Company, 1922)

Chotanka, the Bear Man
Eastman, Charles A., *Indian Boyhood* (Boston: Little, Brown, and Company, 1922)

The Animal People of Devil's Heart
Eastman, Charles A., *Indian Boyhood* (Boston: Little, Brown, and Company, 1922)

The Devil's Tooth
Workers of the Federal Writers Project of the Works Progress Administration for the State of North Dakota, *North Dakota: A Guide to the Northern Prairie State* (Bismarck, ND: State Historical Society of North Dakota, 1938)

Transcript of an interview with Pauline Gray Water, July 21, 1992 by Lance Nixon, Grand Forks Herald staff writer, from the Elwyn B. Robinson Department of Special Collections, Chester Fritz Library, University of North Dakota, Grand Forks, ND

The Little People of Devils Lake
Collections of the State Historical Society of North Dakota, Volume 1 (Bismarck, ND: State Historical Society of North Dakota, 1906)

Kenner, Corrine, "The Curse of Devils Lake," *Fate* magazine, October 1997

The Dead Man's Trail
Horne, Bev and Rhonda Greene, *Totten Mail Trail Riders Tales* (Fort Totten, ND: Friends of Fort Totten Historic Site, 1997)

Workers of the Federal Writers Project of the Works Progress Administration for the State of North Dakota, *North Dakota: A Guide to the Northern Prairie State* (Bismarck, ND: State Historical Society of North Dakota, 1938)

The Hired Man
Cando Pioneer Foundation Museum, Cando, ND

The Murder of the Ward Brothers
"Murder Indictments Dismissed," *The New York Times*, July 18, 1884.

"North Dakota's First Mass Murder" (Fargo, ND: Prairie Public Radio *Dakota Datebook*, July 7, 2004.)

"The Murder of the Ward Boys," *The New York Times*, April 30, 1883.

"The Ward Brothers Buried," *The New York Times*, April 28, 1883.

"The Ward Brothers Tragedy" in *The Early History of the Devils Lake Country* (Larimore, ND: Printed by H. V. Arnold, 1920)

"Two Brothers Murdered: Nephews of C. B. Farwell Killed in a Dakota Land Quarrel." *The New York Times*, April 25, 1883.

Scarff, M. T., "Bartlett's 40th Anniversary—1882-1922." (Devils Lake, ND: Pioneers Association, circa 1926-1933)

The Blizzard Ghost
"A Severe Blizzard," *The New York Times*, February 1, 1887

Follow-up brief, *The New York Times*, February 10, 1887

Horn Cloud's Revenge
"Horn Cloud's Revenge," *The New York Times*, March 21, 1890

The Virgin Feast
Eastman, Charles Alexander, *Old Indian Days* (New York: The S.S. McClure Company, 1907)

The Phantom Ship of Devils Lake
Wyard, J. Morley, in the *Park River Gazette Witness* and quoted in *Devils Lake Illustrated* (Grand Forks, ND: Press of Grand Forks Herald, 1898)

The Day Jack Kenny Lost His Head
"Dog Finds Skull," (Fargo, ND: Prairie Public Radio *Dakota Datebook*, February 21, 2004)

The Devils Lake Sea Serpent
Devils Lake Chamber of Commerce, Devils Lake, N. D.

Skinner, Charles Montgomery, *American Myths and Legends* (Philidelphia: J.B. Lippincott Company, 1903)

Workers of the Federal Writers Project of the Works Progress Administration for the State of North Dakota, *North Dakota: A Guide to the Northern Prairie State* (Bismarck, ND: State Historical Society of North Dakota, 1938)

The War Maiden
Eastman, Charles Alexander, *Old Indian Days* (New York: The S.S. McClure Company, 1907)

The Haunted Train Station
Registration Application Form, United States Department of the Interior National Park Service National Register of Historic Places, Devils Lake Commercial District, filed September 15, 198

The Wreck of the Oriental Express
"A Wrecked Train Burns Up," *Reno Evening Gazette (Nevada)*, April 15, 1907

"G. N. Oriental Express Wrecked," *Winnipeg Free Press (Manitoba)*, April 16, 1907

The Ghosts at the Great Northern Hotel
Registration Application Form, United States Department of the Interior National Park Service National Register of Historic Places, Devils Lake Commercial District, filed September 15, 1989

The Water Witch of the West
Whitney, Caspar, editor, "A Water-Witcher of the Prairies" *The Outing Magazine: The Outdoor Magazine of Human Interest* (New York: The Outing Publishing Company, January 1907)

The Vision of White Thunder
Newell, Cicero, *Indian Stories* (Boston, New York, and Chicago: Silver, Burdett and Company, 1912)

Sister Saint Alfred's Deathbed Revelations
"Fort Totten Tragedy" (Fargo, ND: Prairie Public Radio *Dakota Datebook*, December 27, 2005)

Peterson, Susan C., "Doing 'Women's Work': The Grey Nuns at Fort Totten Indian Reservation, 1874-190" in *North Dakota History: Journal of the Northern Plains Vol. 52, No. 2* (Bismarck, ND: State Historical Society of North Dakota, Spring 1985)

The Edwards House
North Dakota National Guard, Devils Lake, ND

The Lost Tribe of Garske Colony
Bonham, Kevin, "Memories Set in Stone," *Grand Forks Herald*, September 16, 2006

Oleson, Louise, "Early Settlers Honored at Dedication Ceremony," *Devils Lake Journal*, September 18, 2006

Rikoon, J. Sanford, editor, *Rachel Calof's Story: Jewish Homesteader on the Northern Plain* (Bloomington, IN: Indiana University Press)

Schloff, Linda Mack, "And Prairie Dogs Weren't Kosher" Jewish Women in the Upper Midwest Since 1855 (St. Paul: Minnesota Historical Society Press, 1996)

The Sons of Jacob cemetery website, www.sojnorthdakota.org

Trupin, Sophie, *Dakota Diaspora: Memoirs of a Jewish Homesteader* (Lincoln, NE: The University of Nebraska Press, 1984)

Zaleski, John Jr. "In the Shadows of the Past," *ND Horizons* magazine, Spring 1978

The Ghost of the *Minnie H*
Isern, Tom, "Minnie H," *Plains Folk* syndicated column (Fargo: North Dakota State University, June 5, 2003)

Naugle, Heerman J., "The Story of The Minnie H Steamboat on Devils Lake North Dakota," Reprinted in the *Benson County Farmers Press*, May 3, 1995

The Earl of Caithness
Eriksmoen, Curt and Jan, "Earl operated a ranch at Lakota" *The Bismarck Tribune*, January 5, 2008

"Monument Reveals an Earl's Identity," *The New York Times*, July 20, 1914

Queen Victoria's Maid
"Victoria's Maid Tells of Romance That Brought Her to Cabin in U. S.," *The Milwaukee Journal*, September 15, 1930

The Odd Fellows Dance Hall
Hale, Henry *Collections of the State Historical Society of North Dakota, Volume 3* (Bismarck, ND: State Historical Society of North Dakota, 1910)

Registration Application Form, United States Department of the Interior National Park Service National Register of Historic Places, Devils Lake Commercial District, filed September 15, 1989

Buffalo Bones
"American Buffalo" (Fargo, ND: Prairie Public Radio *Dakota Datebook*, December 17, 2003)

Workers of the Federal Writers Project of the Works Progress Administration for the State of North Dakota, *North Dakota: A Guide to the Northern Prairie State* (Bismarck, ND: State Historical Society of North Dakota, 1938)

About the Author

Corrine Kenner specializes in bringing metaphysical subjects down to earth. She's an award-winning writer who was raised on a farm near Devils Lake. Since then, she has traveled the world studying the mysteries of life and death.

Corrine is the author of more than a dozen books on the paranormal, as well as the editor of four anthologies. Her books are available worldwide, and they've been translated into a dozen languages. Corrine herself has been a keynote speaker at international conferences and events in England, Canada, and across the United States.

Corrine's father, Wayne Kenner, was a postal worker, and her mother, Carolyn Kenner, directed the city's childcare center. As a young adult, Corrine lived in Brazil, where she learned Portuguese, and Los Angeles, where she earned a bachelor's degree in philosophy from California State University. She is the mother of four girls, and she and her husband have homes in Devils Lake and Minneapolis.

To contact Corrine, email corrine@corrinekenner.com or visit her website at corrinekenner.com.

Also by Corrine Kenner

Astrology for Writers

Tarot and Astrology

The Wizards Tarot

The Tarot of Physics

Tarot for Writers

Simple Fortunetelling with Tarot Cards

Crystals for Beginners

Tarot Journaling

Tall Dark Stranger: Tarot for Love and Romance

The Epicurean Tarot

Strange But True

Look for Corrine Kenner's books on Amazon.com.
Visit amazon.com/author/corrinekenner for details.

Made in the USA
San Bernardino, CA
09 July 2014